RISE UP
My Beloved

SONIA McLEOD

Rise Up My Beloved
by Sonia McLeod

Printed in the United States of America

ISBN 978-1-6064-7002-2
Ebook: 978-1-6628-0893-7

Unless otherwise indicated, Bible quotations are taken from The King James Version of the Bible.

www.xulonpress.com

May 3, 2022

Connie

He is good! The Lord is good! Be both blessed and encouraged.

With love!

[illegible]

To my husband, Derek.

Together, we will get to the other side with
our family.
We are taking them all, not one will be left
behind.
I love you so much.

Song of Solomon 2:10-11

My beloved spake, and said unto me,
Rise up, my love, my fair one,
and come away.
For, lo, the winter is past,
the rain is over and gone;

In Loving Memory

David Wilkerson

May 19, 1921- April 27, 2011

Dedication

To my Lord and Saviour, Jesus Christ, I want to thank you for my salvation and for changing me one day at a time. You have been my anchor and my everything. You have been the lifter of my head when I was full of shame. You have been my solid rock when all else failed. You have given me favour and blessed me with an incredible family. There is so much you have done for me that I am not able to say it all. My prayer is that through my story others will find what I have found in you. Jesus, I love you.

To my husband, Derek McLeod, you have been the answer to the prayers I made known unto the Lord. I thank the Lord that He heard me and sent you unto me. You are my best friend and an example for many. Thank you for being such a wonderful husband and father. Your love for the Lord and commitment to Him is such a joy. Thank you for working alongside me to complete this book. Thank you for encouraging me and being there for me. I love you.

To my children, Hassan, Hasslina, Kari, Karyl, Kirsten and David, this is my love letter and story for you to keep all your days. Love the Lord with all your heart and soul. The world only dresses itself to make itself seem glamorous, but it is only a veneer. Love the Lord with all your heart and continue to shine His light to the world. Narrow is the gate and difficult is the way which leads to life, and there are few who find it; keep your eyes on Jesus. I love you.

To my mother, upon whom the Son shines, there were days that, it seemed, would never end, but it was your goodness and love that would often pull me through. You never quit on me, but endured along with me. I thank the Lord for blessing me with you. Mom, because of you, I made it.

What are people saying about Rise Up My Beloved?

"When we read this book, we saw the awesome works of God and how He can work with the surrendered Christian. Ministry to the drug addict, alcoholic, and others in similar situations can be discouraging at times. This book has encouraged our faith."

–Reverend Larry & Diane Browning, MI, USA

"Through her many trials, Sonia has remained a model of courage, compassion and faithfulness. She encouraged and inspired my late husband and I in carrying on our ministry to native children through Camp Living Water, a summer Bible camp. Sonia is a true trophy of God's grace! I could not put her book down."

– Jean Stewart, Founder, Camp Living Water Ministries, AB, Canada

"WOW! This book speaks life. It will minister to you. Reading this book has opened my eyes and set me free. Upon finishing this book I made the best decision of my life by accepting Jesus Christ. I am in awe of what He is doing with me already. I am on fire for the Lord!"

– Cheryl Mooswa, SK, Canada

"If God can do this in Sonia's life, He can do it in others. Pray for this book. It will touch many lives."

–Reverend Ernie & Shirley Linklater, Full Gospel Aboriginal Ministries, ON, Canada

Acknowledgements

During the writing of this book, I came to several crossroads that could have discouraged me from finishing the course. There were a number of people that I must thank and acknowledge for their encouragement, prayers, and friendship during this time:

Special thanks to Scott and Yvette Kinley; Your family blessed mine at a time when we were barely hanging on. Your words, your encouragement, your giving, and your lives have shown and taught me much. Thank you so much.

To Jean Stewart and her departed husband Larry whom we all dearly miss; Your unwavering faith, perseverance, and commitment to doing the Lord's will have been such an encouragement and a blessing to witness. Your friendship has been a true blessing.

To Aaron and Jan Siemens; Thank you for your prayers and friendship. Thank you for the blessing you have been to my family. My life has been truly enriched having had you come into my path.

To Bill and Marjorie McLeod; Thank you for raising up the wonderful man who has become my husband. Your prayers and encouragement give me strength every day.

To my friends, Roland and Leanne Gosse, Danielle and Andrew Lampman; Thank you. Your friendship has been a blessing from the Lord.

To Greg Williams; Thank you. Your words of encouragement came at a time when I needed to hear them the most.

Preface

There are three reasons why I decided that I needed to write my story. Firstly, I needed to share of God's amazing love and mercy in my life. I wanted the world, and our native people, to know that He is more than able to reach down to the deepest depths in order to save us. Like the psalmist wrote, even if I make my bed in hell, there You are with me. Secondly, I needed to share about God's incredible and extraordinary grace. His grace far exceeds our understanding and surpasses every possible imagination of our frail human minds. Thirdly, I just could not contain within my soul all that He has done for me. I know that He can do the same for others.

My story is also an exhortation to edify the Church and the body of believers. My hope is that it will bring encouragement and a desire to press in deeper with the Lord. And more so, that, somehow through my story, the backslider would be drawn back into relationship with the Heavenly Father.

Somewhere the time we once spent with the Lord has withered away. Our hearing from Him has grown dim. Sin has taken full reign in our lives and in our churches. More and more we see sin being uncovered and exposed in many ministries. The Word of the Lord says that all the works of man will be tried by fire. Sadly, we see many works and ministries being burned up today. Our churches have now become a joke rather than places of safe refuge that we can run to. Marriages and ministries have been destroyed and brought down by the lust of the flesh, the lust of the eyes, and the pride of life. Will we ever learn that sin destroys?

Yet, the collapse of these things can lead us into the restoration of our heavenly relationship once again! What is important, to this restoration, is that we do not sit under condemnation from either behind the pulpit, or self-condemnation from within. Whatever has been burnt up, we must remember that He, Jesus Christ, is able to turn our ashes into beauty. He will not extinguish a smoldering flame.

No matter what you have done, or where you are, the Lord is waiting for you and is more than able to restore, renew, and keep you. His grace is extraordinary! His love is beyond our understanding. It spreads as far as the east is from the west. It is limitless! Whenever we call upon Him with repentance, no matter how many times we fall, He is there to pick us up again. He does not take away His love from us. His thoughts toward those who love Him are good. He knows everything about us. He knows of our failings and our weaknesses. This is why He came to walk with us, to help us along the way.

There will be many voices ready to condemn and destroy you, including your own. Yet Christ pleads for us to press in. Press in beloved, because He is waiting. Press through the condemning crowd, and the accusing voices, and endure until the end.

Let us return to the Lord once again and love Him. Let us love Him with all our heart and let Him consume our lives once again. We need Him in this dark hour, and in the times that are ahead. Beloved, if you do not know Jesus Christ as Lord and Saviour, accept Him today, and be blessed by His testimony.

~one~

The Overflow of Evil

Revelation 12:12
"Woe to the inhabiters of the earth and of the sea! For the devil is come down unto you, having great wrath, because he knoweth that he hath but a short time."

August 29, 2001, London, Ontario

It was a beautiful day. I had to head downtown and run some errands. I decided to take the kids with me on the bus. The kids always loved the bus ride. We were looking forward to a wonderful day.

On the way to the bus stop the kids and I noticed a helicopter circling above us. I knew that the police were obviously looking for someone. The first thing that came to my mind was a car pursuit, or a robbery, but it was obviously something bad. It wasn't until we got on the bus that we learned what was taking place. We overheard the crackle of the radio as the bus driver was informed about a missing little girl. The dispatcher gave a description of the little girl and had been told by police to be on the lookout.

When I had finally settled in with the kids, I took this time to explain to my children what was happening and encouraged them to always stay close. It was difficult to believe this was happening. Our community was hit by a blow of reality that bad things can happen anywhere and strike at any time. My heart went out to her family and thinking about how scared they must be. Hopefully, she was just lost and would be found soon.

By the time we got home that afternoon from our trip downtown, the search had been called off. Her lifeless body had been found. The evening news reported that a suspect was in custody. What we would learn a few short hours later would shake our home.

When the suspect's name was mentioned in the news, we were in complete disbelief. It was a name we all knew. A boy, whom I loved like a brother, had raped and murdered this beautiful and innocent five year old girl. My mom called me from work and whispered his name into the phone; she was in shock too. I raced downstairs where my brother lay on the sofa and told him what I had heard. He jumped up not knowing how to react or what to say. The only thought that ran through both of our minds was 'this has to be a mistake!'

How does something like this happen? This can't be happening! How Lord?

My mind was running through a million thoughts a minute. What was going to happen next? His mother, a Christian woman and my mother's best friend, was a wonderful and amazing woman whom I held dear to my heart. How can this be? Whenever I needed someone to talk to she was always there and always made the time to listen. She was a woman I loved with all my heart and a woman I admired. All I could think was 'How is she even possibly handling this?'

It all just seemed so unreal. It was like a horrible nightmare that you just want to wake up out of. How could this horrific tragedy happen to the family of such a wonderful woman? *Lord, Oh God, help her and help the family of this little girl.*

I found myself in the days that followed in a dazed, almost dreamlike, state. Nothing seemed real. It was hard to accept. The thought lingered that 'maybe they made a mistake.' This just could not be! When the news of it settled in and the horror of the details were known, I wept. I was left wondering how such evil could invade and consume someone. I was lost for words. Sadly, I was losing any fading hope I had for humanity. *Where did it all go wrong?*

Soon afterward came the fear. It seemed to invade every moment of my life. Horrific images would flash through my mind. I began checking, double-checking, and even triple-checking the locks and windows. I was a single parent and I was becoming paranoid. I would often wonder who was watching us.

This was a boy I knew and trusted. I loved and considered his family like my own. Whatever could happen in a person's mind to possess them to do such evil things? The thought was frightening and it sent shivers down my back. This beautiful angelic little girl was brutally taken away. Dread filled my heart when I thought to remember that just recently he had been at my house looking for my brother. I was looking forward to our next visit with him. I had been expecting to see a lot more of him since he hung around with my brothers. I loved him like my own brother. I would have opened my house for him at any time. Now my heart sank with the reality of evil and the many faces evil can wear. And some of those faces could be so close to our own homes.

My heart ached for the parents of this little girl. I could only imagine their grief, how would they endure? Precious. Adorable. She was a little girl who brought so much laughter and joy to those around her and to her parents. But now instead of embracing her, they would have to hear and relive the horrific and evil details of what had been so viciously done to her.

Lord, have mercy on us…

~two~

The Lifter of My Head

Psalm 3:3
But you, oh Lord, are a shield for me, my glory and the one who lifts up my head.

It was now autumn 2002 and I was interested in finding a good Bible College – it didn't matter where I went – my only desire at this point in my life was to go. It was the only thing I wanted to do. I wanted to breathe and learn the Word of God. Then one evening, as I sat at my computer desk, the Lord began to stir feelings in my heart that I had learned to suppress over time.

My walk with Jesus was becoming more intimate. He was beginning to show me the hard places in my heart. Like the story about the clay in the potter's hand, there were hardened areas in my heart that Christ needed to tear down and lovingly shape me into a vessel that could be used for His glory (Jeremiah 18:1-6). Feelings of shame, bitterness and hatred needed to be torn down. In the process of this, His love filled my inner being. For so long I had been ashamed of being a First Nations woman and as I sat there thinking, going back as far as I could remember, I had always been ashamed of my cultural heritage. My blonde streaks and the constant changes to my looks and my wardrobe were devices I used to reflect someone else. (There is nothing wrong in change and changing hair color. I was merely masking who I was).

I felt that if I admitted I was an Indian, I was admitting I was an alcoholic. Somewhere along the way I came to believe the enemy's lie: *First Nations people are second class citizens*. He had caused me to believe that I could never be enough. But I had a Deliverer who knew every dark place and could set me free from the enemy and his lies.

Isaiah 42:7 NKJV
To open blind eyes, to bring out prisoners from the prison, those who sit in darkness from the prison house.

This weight I had been carrying was finally lifted. My burden was gone! This breakthrough was critical for my walk with the Lord. This helped me to understand that First Nation's people were God's people too. He died for them as much as anyone else. It was for my sin, and for the sin within all men that He had died. This went a lot deeper than the racial barriers I ever felt. All along, my race had made no difference to Christ.

I now knew who I was in Christ. Knowing that Christ died for me when I wasn't worth it, and when I didn't deserve it, was important. His love for me was astronomical and there wasn't anything I could do to make Him love me more or less. This healing touch I received from the Lord was breathtaking! I loved Him more because of it.

Now free, I wanted to run to every house on the reserve to tell them what Christ did for me! I wanted to declare to my native people, *'There is a God and He loves you! This Jesus is real! He is here right in the midst of us and all you have to do is believe.'* I wanted to go and shake some up and say, *"Don't you feel Him?"* This presence that stirred in my heart was real. This love from within was beginning to overflow – I wanted to get to the highest mountain top and shout it!

I knew that night that I was being called into the ministry. I knew that if only one should come to know the truth and be set free from sin, then everything I shared would be worth it. It was at this point in my life the Lord impressed on my heart to start writing. I was to share all that the Lord did and all that He was going to do. I remember the battle that I was engaged in with my mind and in my heart. *Who was I? And who was going to listen to me? How could someone like me make a difference?* The Lord reminded me that it wasn't anything I was going to do – it was going to be by His Spirit.

Zachariah 4:6
"...Not by might nor by power, but by my spirit" ...

Although inspired and challenged to share my testimony, I was hesitant. I thought of family and friends finding out about me and the shame it would bring. However, the more I drew closer to the Lord, I found out He didn't come to condemn me or bring me to shame. He loved me unconditionally and it would be the cross and the shedding of His blood that would change me. I was a new creation! (2 Corinthians 5:17) It was going to be my testimony that would encourage others and set others free. Jesus brought the Word of God so that we may have life and live it more abundantly.

~three~

Called to Testify for Him

Isaiah 49:16

See, I have inscribed you on the palms of My hands; Your walls are continually before Me.

My Beginning

My parents, Joy Kennedy and Steve Webster, were anxiously waiting for my arrival. It was two weeks after my due date. The day I decided to start my earthly journey, my mom was at the Indian Affairs office seeking financial assistance. With plans on living together to support their first child, my parents needed help. They wanted to find a house, but they were unable to afford rental costs. So it was decided that they would get help from Indian Affairs. Indian Affairs provided services to First Nation people, or "Indians", much like social welfare does today. Both my parents were very young, my mom was 15; my dad was 17 years old.

It was on the day my mom went in to the Indian Affairs office that I decided to make my appearance. Mom thought she was just having a bad stomach ache. She sat in her chair, rocking back and forth, across from her social worker. He took notice and asked her when she was due. She stated she was already two weeks late. He quickly issued her a cheque and advised her to immediately go to the hospital. Instead, she went to her sister's house. It didn't take long before her older sister took notice and called their mother. My mother's older brother came by to pick her up and he dropped her off at the hospital.

June 24, 1974

In the hospital room, alone and afraid, she was faced with the reality that she was going to have a baby. She started to cry. An older native lady who had been in the room observing came forward to talk to her. She asked my mother if it was the pain that was causing her to cry. "No," my mother replied, "this isn't the reason." Then this kindly elderly woman asked "Are you alone?" "Yes, I am," was my frightened mother's answer.

This was not the way I'm sure she wanted it, but there she was, alone and scared with her first child on the way. It was then that this angel of a woman, whoever she was, reached out and held my mother's hand. Thankfully she did what she did because my mother needed to go to the washroom and this woman was able to prevent my mother from doing so. When my mother got up to go, this native woman pushed my mother back into her seat and told her to stay seated while she went and got the nurse. I was already in the birthing canal and ready to come out. It was a good thing my mother hadn't gone to the bathroom or I would have had a cold and nasty wet surprise.

The delivery went well and I made my entrance into this world. The air was cold, but besides being a bit uncomfortable, I was a healthy baby girl. After mom had time to recuperate, she had wanted to thank this beautiful woman who had helped her, but she was nowhere to be found. Today, we know she was from the Lord; she had come to give mom hope and comfort. And it had made all the difference in the world.

My dad arrived sometime later. He had tried to be there earlier, but different circumstances wouldn't allow that. My parents stayed together for a few months after my birth and then separated. I was given over to *Kokum* (my grandmother) who would be awarded custody of me. Soon after, my father left. Any relation I had with my dad ceased for a while and for many years thereafter. My dad left and pursued Bible College. He later married. My mother had started drinking and had no desire to become a pastor's wife. Although being a pastor's wife wasn't what she wanted she can recall a moment she had one day while holding me in her arms. She knew in her heart that the Lord was going to use me one day… How? When? She didn't know, but it didn't matter, she was given some small hope to hold on to. Very young and on her own my mother continued partying. I witnessed a lot of things that many native children endure on a daily basis. When I was about the age of two, my mom went to court and regained custody of me. I continued to stay with *Kokum*, however, on weekends and during holidays. She was like a second mom to me. She loved me and wanted only the very best for me.

For my mom and I, however, violence and heartache seemed to follow us. I witnessed mom getting physically abused and I was sexually abused twice. The first time was by my mother's boyfriend. I didn't breathe a word of it to my mom until I was 16 yrs old and intoxicated. The second incident was by my aunt's boyfriend. I was about eight years old. Once it was settled in court, he was given only six months. For many years later, I could still hear the heavy breathing and feel their hands on me. Both of these sexual assaults left their dreadful mark on me. They would trigger within me a promiscuous lifestyle and lead me into unhealthy relationships.

Kokum provided me the comfort and care I needed as a child. She was always very protective of me. I loved her with all my heart. I can remember so many good times I had with her, grocery shopping and going to work with her. I enjoyed sitting with her late in the evenings while she told stories. We would laugh and talk until late into the night. She loved me so much and for this I will always be grateful. She was an amazing lady and very special. She taught me a lot and encouraged me to complete my education. She worked hard and achieved a lot and she wanted the same things for her children and for me. I could always call her. We could always laugh together. Or she would give me the hard truth about the direction of my life when I was heading down a wrong path.

Kokum was a woman of great strength. She fought and advocated for native rights and she was someone no one dared to argue with unless they knew what they were talking about. She was the first woman elected as a native chief in Canada. She always told me to push ahead in life and pursue my dreams regardless of who believed in me. My grandmother was one of a kind! Sadly, I lost my grandmother on August 10, 2005. She has gone home to be with the Lord. I miss her greatly.

My mother had married a native man from the Oneida Settlement in Ontario; they met and married in Edmonton, Alberta. It was at this point in my mother's life that she quit drinking. I liked our stepfather. He was a good provider. On the surface our step-dad seemed to accept my brother and me, but it was my younger brother Shaun who got the short end of our step-dad's temper. He had a short fuse when it came to Shaun. This was upsetting to my mom and me, but nonetheless, he was the head of the house. Then came the births of my two youngest brothers. Now there were three children in the house, well four, including me. Yet, I always had *Kokum*.

When *Kokum* had moved out to Key Indian reserve in Saskatchewan from Edmonton, Alberta, I was around nine years old. She enrolled me in the elementary school in the neighbouring community of Canora, Saskatchewan. Things were going good. It wasn't long afterward that we received a phone call. It was my mom.

Up until *Kokum* and I had moved, mom and *Kokum* had been living in Edmonton. It had been easy to split my time between *Kokum* and my mother. But now that I was living on the reserve with *Kokum* I did not get to see my mother very often. Although I loved *Kokum*, it was hard not having my mom nearby. Mom was calling to know if I wanted to move with my siblings, her husband, and with her to Ontario. I remember the devastation I felt. I wanted to stay with *Kokum*, but wanted my mother too. *Kokum* sat down to talk with me and I knew she understood that I wanted to go. I needed my mother. I felt so torn... I'll never forget our dinner at the bus depot in Yorkton, Saskatchewan on the day I boarded the bus for Ontario. I remember feeling anxious and scared because I wasn't sure when I would be back again. I was heading somewhere for a new start. I had no idea of the pain that laid ahead for me.

When I first heard the name London, Ontario, it sounded like another country and so far away. My brothers were too young to understand what was going on. We were leaving "home" and I was the only one upset.

My stepfather always worked hard, my mom seemed happy for a while. Once we settled in London, I started going to school and eventually made some friends. Things weren't that bad. I missed *Kokum* a lot and worried about her because she was alone. I told her whenever she became old and needed to be looked after I would come back to care for her as long as I wasn't married with children. We stayed in touch and I opened a bank account so she could send me money from time to time, as long as I stayed in school. We missed each other a lot, but it was time we let go of each other.

~four~

Lost in Sin and Found by Christ

Romans 10:13
For whosoever shall call upon the name of the Lord shall be saved.

My mom had started going to church and my brothers and I attended Sunday school and began to learn about God. We began to hear about this man named Jesus Christ.

One summer, our church sent the children to camp and a lady from our congregation paid for my fees to go. The experience and the impact this camp had on me, I believe, saved my life. Memories of this summer would surface time and time again throughout my life. It was through this camp that I found out that this gospel and the things they preached at church about Jesus was, and is, real. One evening at camp I watched as they performed a skit of how He was crucified.

God would send his only begotten son, Jesus, into the world to save it. Men were being bound by satan, an evil and wicked pied piper. Satan lured men with riches to build bigger palaces, bigger kingdoms, and more power, while their hearts waxed worse and worse. Satan held and blinded men in captivity. It was for this cause, Christ came.

2 Corinthians 4:4 NKJV
Whose minds the god of this age has blinded, who do not believe, lest the light of the gospel of the glory of Christ, who is the image of God, should shine on them.

Christ full of compassion and love for humanity would bring forth a plan of redemption; to restore and bring forth riches to enter the heart. Christ Jesus knew that in death and by His resurrection, those who believed in Him would be given the Holy Spirit (Acts 2:38). He would lead and guide us into all truth. Man would be given power over all the power of the enemy and would no longer be bound. He, Jesus, did this so that we may abound with eternal life full of love, freedom, joy, and peace.

John 3:16
For God so loved the world that He gave His only begotten Son, that whosoever believeth in Him should not perish but have everlasting life.

No more would men have to taste of death and be consumed by satan, but now, men could choose to rise with Christ into glory. Christ would come and be our example. It was going to be the love of Christ within the heart of men that would keep them. It would be a choice.

Jesus was born and dwelt among His people and at the appointed time He went out and preached the gospel. There were many religious leaders who were in authority that wanted Jesus destroyed. Embedded in their souls were pride, envy, and rebellion and this sin in their hearts rose up against Him. It seemed wherever this Jesus went, people listened and wherever Jesus walked He changed lives. He healed lives that were sick by disease or in torment. He was a light; one who brought hope, future, a promise, and new life.

Then, as a thief in the night, they came to Him. Led by one of His own disciples, He would be betrayed by a kiss. They grabbed Him and His beatings and torment began as His blood spilled. They continued to whip Him over and over again until His flesh became raw. They spared Him no mercy. As Christ looked into the crowd, He watched one of His beloved disciples deny Him – as He said he would – a third time.

The crowd hated His goodness, His compassion, and His mercy. They hated everything He stood for. They stood laughing, mocking, and ridiculing Him. Someone in the crowd screamed "If you are the Son of God, defend yourself!" And yes, at anytime He could have called ten thousand angels to His side.

But all this was just the vile manifestation of what was in the heart of men. And yet, in the midst of all this pain, He would never answer them with the wrath they deserved.

Then they placed a crown of thorns onto His head. Soaked in His own blood, His divine body and head reeled with pain. They made Him carry His cross, thirsty and tired, while bystanders continued to jeer and scream at Him. He could feel all the evil and wickedness as it was thrust into His face. Every part of His body screamed in pain. Seeing your face and mine, and the many children who need Him, He endured, that in Him, they might live.

And then, at the hill of Calvary, they hammered the nails into His hands and His feet. Now, nailed to the cross, they mocked our King by hanging a cruel note above His head that read "King of the Jews." But He, full of grace and mercy, beholding His Father's promise unto all generations, cried out "Father, forgive them, for they know not what they do."

After the skit was finished, I could feel the presence of the Lord among us. They gave an altar call to come forward to accept Jesus Christ. Many came forward, including me. I can remember the tears rolling down my face as the sweet presence of the Lord filled the room. I accepted Jesus into my life that evening. I desired to know this great King and this amazing God who died in my place. I opened my heart to Him and invited Him to come live in me. As I lifted my hands to surrender, my mouth poured forth an utterance from Heaven. The presence of the Lord was upon me and it was an experience that would forever stay with me. It was far beyond any words I could express. I knew that night there really was a God and no one could make me believe otherwise.

~five~

Crumbling, Shaken, and Divided

Psalm 127:1
Except the LORD build the house, they labour in vain that build it:

My family stayed in London for a couple of years and my step-dad moved us out to the Oneida Settlement. He didn't like us kids in the city, and he especially watched over me like a protective father. Although he wasn't my biological father he was always good to me.

Living on the reserve took some time getting used to, but I soon made friends and things were good for a while. My mom continued serving the Lord. I could see the change that God had made in my mother. It was undeniable; God had changed her into a wonderful and caring mother. But I can recall a time being so furious and so upset with her because she wouldn't allow me to go to my grade eight graduation. I thought she was going a little too far with this whole God thing.

The relationship between my mother and I was relatively good; she was a good mother to us kids. She liked to dress me in the finest clothes. I can remember days coming home from school to find new clothes on my bed. I always had what I needed and, even sometimes, got what I wanted. She taught me early on how to work; I always had chores. She instilled in me fine qualities and she kept me up on my studies at school. She would have me reading in my room before going to bed at night. I guess now I know why I love to read. I loved my mother and this would be one of the last few good memories I would have with her before things changed for all of us.

The Tide Begins to Turn

It was maybe a year later when things in the house started to change. I could feel tension in the house between my step-dad and mother. Fear would rise up in my stomach and I feared my mother would be hit or beaten. He had never become physical with my mom, but I knew something was wrong. One day, after coming home from school, my mom had everything packed up and ready to go. My step-dad was at work and had no clue that my mom was leaving him. I remember feeling very nervous, but we left without incident.

We went to London and stayed with a friend of my mom. She took us in until we were able to find a place. We had already been at the shelter, but my younger brothers were a handful and mom had a hard time keeping them under control so we had to leave the shelter. It wasn't too long before we were settled in our own home. Mom moved us into a townhouse, southeast of London. It was a nice place. Mom did residential cleaning to keep food on the table. Although things were at times chaotic, mom worked hard to keep us clothed and fed. I thought things were going good.

It was around this time that the police started showing up at our door for things my brothers did. My brothers were feeling the absence of their dad and they were acting out these feelings in a destructive way. Everything seemed a mess. Things were changing.

One day, feeling so overwhelmed, my mom called their dad and told him to come pick up my brothers. They didn't want to go; they cried and begged to stay. My brother Otto grabbed on to my mother's leg and begged to stay. I can only imagine how they cried, pleaded, and promised to be good… but she made them go, figuring it was best for them. They were too young to understand why they were leaving, but having their father and his provision seemed more promising for them at the time. I know it broke my mother's heart. It broke mine too, but more than anything else it made me angry. I missed my brothers so much and I know my mom did too. In an attempt to escape the pain and guilt my mother picked up the bottle.

I became a bitter and angry young girl – I didn't understand anything either.

Although I was in school it was becoming harder to stay in school. Mom would party throughout the night and it was like she just gave up on my other brother and I.

Our home just wasn't home without the boys and we missed them. I was just a child, I didn't understand; the life I knew wasn't going to be the same anymore. In my frame of mind, all I saw in my mom was someone who just wanted to party. She soon became someone I despised. I would watch her drinking and carrying on. How I hated her! Now, being a mother myself, I know my mother's heart was broken. Her two babies were gone, her marriage and everything she had hoped for was gone. There was no one she could talk to who could minister life. Maybe one day she would find her way again, but for now, everything was too much. She had given up.

~six~

Seeking A Way Out

John 10:10

The thief does not come except to steal, and to kill, and to destroy. I have come that they may have life, and that they may have it more abundantly.

My mother changed overnight. Our home which used to be spotless was now always a mess. Beer bottles could be found strewn throughout our home at any time. In the midst of this I became the caregiver for my other brother, Shaun. I fed and helped care for him. It was a difficult time – for all of us. I know my brother felt neglected and uncared for. And for this I despised my mother even more.

The relationship between my mom and I was not a good one. I didn't like my mom. My feelings for her grew worse and worse. We did a lot of arguing and fighting. I would curse and say things in anger to her that I would not even think to say to anyone today.

As a teenager, I had my first boyfriend, Clive. He and I were together for a couple of years. He was good to me. He loved me. It was me who did not know how to love him in return. I was so angry. All I knew to do was fight. If we weren't fighting, I would start a fight. My mind was messed up. I had conformed to the ways that I had been brought up. I was full of anger and bitterness. This was poisoning the happiness – and everything – that I wanted. Clive gave me all the things a young girl could want, but still, something was missing. I still wasn't happy.

I hated who I had become. I wanted to love Clive and show him I cared. Instead I did all the things I hated. I hurt him over and over again. I would hit him and throw things at him. I remember one night while we were having an argument, Clive, who didn't want to argue, started to leave. Rather than let him leave, I grabbed the closest thing to me and threw it at him. It hit him in the head and knocked him to the ground. As he laid there on the ground, I stood over him, screaming at him. I would later cry because I didn't know what was wrong with me.

Clive tried so hard, over and over again, but nothing made me happy. New gifts, an apartment, car, money to spend; what I wanted, he purchased. Yet I wasn't happy. I would cause an argument just because I wanted to and I would say things to make him angry. If he wasn't angry, I would find ways to make him angry.

One night we had a big fight, and as I often would do being my psychotic self, I left the apartment angry. It was during this time that Clive called his parents. When I arrived back at the apartment, his parents were there to drive me to my mother's home. Clive had called it quits. When he had finally realized he couldn't change me, he quit trying. He had grown tired of trying. It was obvious to him that I wasn't going to change. Things were really over. I was devastated. I remember pleading with him in the bedroom. Although it was hard for both of us, I knew this was it. I'll never forget that night when his parents drove me to my mother's house. I packed my things and grabbed a hold of my new puppy he had just bought for me a few days before. When I got to my mother's place, she was partying. I went straight up to my old room and cried … and cried. Oh, how my heart hurt. I had no one. Realizing that, I hurt even more.

My mother didn't seem to care about me. And where was my father? If he loved me, wouldn't he call me or stay in touch with me? I knew my dad was a preacher, a man of God, and somehow along the way, I had been forgotten. I knew my parents loved me, but even when I didn't understand what or why things were happening, the Lord was taking care of me. Sometimes, even though they may have good intentions, those who love us will fail us.

Psalm 27:10 NKJV
When my father and mother forsake me, then the Lord will take care of me.

Nevertheless with all the hurt and nowhere to turn, I was going to run and do the things I wanted to do. No one could have stopped me, except the arms of the one I wanted; but they were no longer there for me. I was going to run while I could, until I found what I was looking for – someone to love me. I would soon find out that the only arms I could run to, and be safe in, were the arms of my Saviour Jesus Christ.

That night after drying my eyes, I got up and settled it in my own heart that I too was going to start drinking. It just seemed like the only thing to do.

Sweet Sixteen – Suicide!
June 24, 1990

It was my birthday. My sweet 16 – at least it should have been. Mom had ordered me a clown. I couldn't believe it! I had to sit there until he was done singing "Happy Birthday." I was so depressed.

Nothing could have cheered me up. My younger brothers who were over visiting were the only ones who seemed to enjoy the clown. They were happy, but I just didn't care for the clown. I just got more and more annoyed with this obnoxious clown prancing around. I sat there, miserable, waiting until he finished singing my birthday song. I was so heartbroken over losing Clive. He was the only one that cared about me and I had pushed him away. I hated myself. I hated everything about my life. I did not want to live life without Clive. And no stupid clown was going to change the fact I had pushed Clive away.

Devastated by my loss, I went through the house looking for my mother's medication. I was going to end it. I was determined to die. I swallowed any medication I could find. I grabbed a glass of water and started ingesting a few at a time until they were all gone. The room started to spin and my vision began to blur. Staggered by the pills I decided to lie down on my bed. Death was setting in. My foolish determination was about to be rewarded. But thank God my mom decided to check on me. She saw the pill container beside my bed and knew exactly what I had done.

In my semi-conscious and extremely groggy state, mom grabbed me and rushed me to the hospital. I barely remember anything from that point. My mom told me that they pumped my stomach full of charcoal. I can remember the doctor asking me to count his fingers – I was ok. They admitted me into the psychiatric ward so that they could keep an eye on me and keep me from trying to commit suicide again. My mother contacted my dad and I can remember someone coming to pray for me on his behalf. Maybe he did care for me... but he still didn't come. I would have liked to have seen him, but when I knew he wasn't coming my heart became more bitter and hard.

Something happened during my short stay in the hospital. My death wish was gone – I now wanted to live. But what I wanted to live for was to party. After being locked up in the hospital for almost a week, I decided I had to leave. But because I was being watched I had to plan an escape.

My cousin, who was just a few years younger than I was, came by to visit me. His visit cheered me up. My plan for escape was simple. I got my cousin to grab my clothes and we simply left the hospital. The next step of the plan was equally simple – find a party! It was Friday and we were going to find a party. When I arrived home, mom was already drunk. The hospital phoned to notify my mom that I had left the hospital, but I didn't stay long at the apartment for fear that someone would come after me.

Broken, Running, and Searching

I didn't take education seriously. I attended high school part-time and the rest of the time I would be fighting; giving a licking or taking a licking. It didn't matter to me either way. I had this hard exterior that seemed rough and tough, but inwardly, I was hurting. I continued school until Grade 10, and then dropped out. I just wanted to fight and drink.

My mom reminded me of a time when one night, while drinking, my mom turned and told me that when the day should come that I stand behind the pulpit, she hoped that my face would not be scarred up; or worse, that I wouldn't be sitting in a wheel-chair. In my mind, she couldn't have been farther from the truth. She was living in her own dreams. I would never stand behind a pulpit. I thought she was crazy for saying so. I went on and carried on my own business of partying. I would leave home for days and it didn't matter to me. I would go for weeks from one party to another. I would hitchhike to Toronto to find a party and always found one. It didn't matter to me where I found a party – all that mattered was that I found one. I didn't care with who, or where the party was. I was walking a dangerous path and I didn't care.

~seven~

A Point of No Return

Psalm 139:8
...if I make my bed in hell, behold, thou art there.

It was on one of my travels to Toronto that my life took a turn down a dark and dangerous path. As I was walking through the downtown center, I met some girls who were not much older than I was. They were busy shopping and they looked like they were having fun. I was drawn to them. I quickly introduced myself and we all hit it off. After some time, they invited me back to their hotel; they had someone for me to meet. I figured it out fast – these girls were street workers. They were prostitutes. And it wasn't long before I found myself joining them.

It seemed that I reached a point of no return; I wasn't dealing with just anyone anymore. This was real, and looking back, I stopped feeling and lived for the moment and never thought of tomorrow. I remember one of the two girls that befriended me told me she had everything she could have possibly wanted, and her parents were rich. However, I could see the pain in her eyes; they were familiar to what I felt in my own heart. I was not the only one dying inside.

Later that night, I was walking the stroll of downtown Toronto. How far I had fallen from where I once was. I was now prostituting myself. It wasn't what I was looking for, but who was going to stop me? I had longed for someone to hold and love me. So here I was. I had no value for who I was. What I was doing now did not matter to me. My heart was hard. What I was doing was frightening and scary. But now, my choice was made, this was my life.

One night, at an after hours club we would frequent, I narrowly escaped a date with eternity. I had had too much to drink. In fact, I do not remember what happened until I was told about it later. My pimp, Johnny, had come to my aid. He knew that I had had more than enough alcohol. He wanted me to leave. I was his girl, and whatever he wanted, I was to do as I was told. However, when I refused to go he picked me up, threw me over his shoulder, and carried me out. It was only a few hours later that a drug deal went bad. The result was gunfire. I could have been caught in the crossfire. Who knows if I could have entered eternity that night?

When Johnny and I heard about this, he told me to get off the block and told me that I deserved more – and this was coming from a pimp! But, I wasn't ready to give up my party life. I had too much hidden inside and I wanted it to stay hidden. It was easier to stay drunk so I wouldn't feel anything. I didn't want to feel anything anymore because I didn't care.

The last time I saw Johnny was on the subway, and despite his concern for my life, I walked away from him. I wasn't ready to quit my way of life.

I hope that our paths will cross again. To this day, I still think of Johnny. He was sent to me and although it wasn't for long, his goodness and words of life, brought a little hope for me. Although I didn't go with him, I heard his words for years.

I remember another night where Johnny came to my aid. Some woman on the block, who I had never met before, had tried to hurt me. She had tried to draw me into an alley. But something about her invitation just did not sit right with me. So I refused and left. It was later I found out that she had meant to hurt me. Realizing this I told Johnny about it. He sent word out on her and I didn't see her again. I don't know what happened to her, but it didn't occur to me then, how much the Lord used Johnny to keep me safe.

It seemed that my life was always in danger from one week to the next. A week after almost being attacked, my life would be in danger once again. A taxi pulled up where I was working. A man sat in the back and invited me in. Although I immediately felt a sense of danger, I brushed it aside and jumped in the cab.

We arrived at our destination which turned out to be a dingy motel. Immediately, I started feeling very nervous. I knew something was wrong, something wasn't right. When we arrived in the room, he had a friend waiting. We came in and the man who picked me up emptied his pockets on the table, displaying a lot of cash and drugs. Throughout the night, he had traffic in and out of the room while we smoked. I'm not sure what I had consumed through the night, but as daylight broke through the darkness, I decided it was time to go. I reached for the door. That was when I saw the knife. He held it up to my throat and demanded my money, but even with the blade to my throat, I wasn't giving it up. He could have taken my life right then and there. To me, it wouldn't have mattered anyway. For whatever reason, he withdrew his knife.

Unbeknownst to me, my mother had been awakened from sleep that very night. This was truly God intervening in my life. My mother was a backslidden Christian. She was living a precarious and rebellious lifestyle. But that night God shook her out of sleep. Immediately, I came to her mind. Fear gripped her heart and she fell to her knees and cried out to the Lord to spare my life. It was on this night that my life was spared.

My mother had been worried about me. I was 17 years old and still living at home and I hadn't been home in a couple of weeks. She hadn't heard from me and she had already phoned the police to report me missing. She told a friend that if she didn't hear from me by Mother's Day she knew that I was dead.

One morning, while walking down a familiar Toronto street, I found a phone booth and called my mother collect. I didn't know what day it was. I didn't even know which month it was. I dialed the numbers not knowing what to expect or hear. The phone rang and then I heard my mom's voice on the other end. I had had no idea that the morning I called was Mother's Day. My mom's prayers were being heard and answered. It was later I found out how the Lord spared my life and how He had awoken my mother to pray.

Sometime later, and I don't recall how, I came into contact with the police. They had my missing person's report that my mother had filed. They boarded me on a bus back to London. I didn't look back. I wasn't returning to Toronto. I was going home.

My next couple of years would include more failed relationships involving abuse and more disappointments. I was looking for the love and security I so desperately needed. Somehow, I believed that having a man in my life would make things better. I didn't like being alone. Being alone was scary for me. However, I couldn't trust anyone neither. Somehow in my mind I believed they would eventually hurt me anyway. I was very bitter and this caused me to be angry most of the time. My insecurities, and who I had become, had me believing that no one could love me. I felt alone. No one in the world seemed to care I was dying inside. I merely existed, I wasn't alive. My vision of a knight in shining white armour coming to rescue me was growing extremely dim.

After just a few short days of rest I was off again from home. I was back in the clubs. It wasn't long before I became involved with someone who would almost take my life.

I met a man from Trinidad. I moved in with him and thought what we had was love. Within a short time, he started to become physical with me. I tried to end the relationship, but he wouldn't let me go so easily. We had been living in Brampton, Ontario and once he started becoming physical with me I moved back to London, Ontario and moved in with a friend.

He wanted me back badly. One night, I agreed he could come over so we could talk. He arrived at the apartment with some beer and wine. We were hoping for a good night together. Instead, we began to argue. And I wasn't going to relent. Things were over and I wanted him to leave. He decided he wasn't going to leave and told me to call the police. So I did. I called the police and I told them the situation. They were on their way.

The argument intensified and it became explosive. At one point he lunged at me threatening he was going to put a knife in me if I didn't shut up. I continued shouting at him. He flew towards me, grabbing me to pull me into the kitchen. I screamed and fought to get away. I had managed to get into the hall of my apartment, but before I could run, he caught me and dragged me back into the apartment. He dragged me back into the kitchen. I struggled with him on the floor. And suddenly, before I could process everything that was happening to me at that moment, he was holding a bottle over my head. I didn't know until sometime later that during this fight for my life, there was a police K-9 unit down the block who had heard my screams. They came running, as well as the other police officers whom I had called earlier. Before I knew what was happening, the police surrounded us and drew out their weapons, and commanded him to drop his weapon. He released the bottle he had held over my head and it fell to the floor. All I heard next was the groaning that came out of his mouth in great sobs as he cried on the floor.

I knew I was playing with fire. I was not only witnessing how serious things were getting, but I was also becoming its victim. My clothes were ripped, and I was bleeding from different cuts I suffered while struggling to get away from him. He was charged and I received my subpoena papers to appear in court. Unfortunately, I had already decided I wasn't going to court. His charges were dropped, and I was picked up later for failing to appear. Shortly thereafter, I was slapped with a peace bond because I had threatened his life.

Regrettably, I went to a club one night. He was there and I felt nothing but contempt for him. In my intoxicated state, I got up in his face. My anger, mixed with the alcohol, came to a boiling point and I threatened his life. He was going to pay for what he tried to do. I was still playing with fire. I left the club that night and I never saw him again, but heard from him a year later.

What amazes me is the deceptive lie that comes forward to make us believe that we are somehow indestructible. We have no control over our lives, it's only the Lord that gives life and takes it. We are in His hand and it's only by His mercy and grace that we live; and for His grace and mercy I will be forever grateful. I'm so thankful I never died out there in my sin. The Lord is good.

Christmas was nearing. The phone rang and I answered it. It was him. I was shocked. He told me he knew where I lived, and what I was doing. He wanted me to know that he was right when he said I wasn't going to be anything or go anywhere in my life. Maybe at that point in my life he was right, but it didn't matter. I didn't care what anyone thought. I hung up the phone and that was that.

How did he know so much about my life? I don't know and maybe I'll never know. I was already involved with someone as I'm sure he probably knew. It was very eerie and a little scary. I hadn't been at this place for very long when he called. My phone number was listed in my friend's name. I never would have guessed he knew anything about me.

Did he know everything I was doing until then? It seemed so. At that moment he was right – my life was not going anywhere! My life had slipped further downhill and I'm sure he was sitting there, gloating in his predictions as I slipped further away from reality.

~eight~

Death in a Pipe

Proverbs 15:3
The eyes of the LORD are in every place, beholding the evil and the good.

I had started hanging around in the east end of London with my friend Dee who I had moved in with. She loved to party and she was a lot of fun. I found out she turned tricks on the side to pay her rent and this was how she survived.

I moved in with her and soon we were both working the strip together. The strip was a place that crawled with drug addicts and prostitutes.

Within weeks, I knew all the local dealers and the people on the block. I had made a friend who had worked the street for years and who was an intravenous drug user. One night while we were out, and after scoring a hit, we went into one of the main drug houses to go do our thing. My friend, whose preference was the needle, had just finished shooting up and I had not yet had any. I wasn't one for needles, but that night it didn't matter. I needed a hit bad. I was just about to ask for her needle when another girl came in and took it. It was only weeks later the news circulated on the block that my friend had AIDS.

I couldn't believe how close I had come to contracting this disease, and if I had had my way that evening, I would have freely received it. The last time I saw her was in the alleyway waiting for clients to come. I hugged her and told her things would be ok. I didn't know what else to say. I didn't know it was going to be one of the last times I would see her.

It was during this time on the strip that I met T-Bone.

T-Bone was the all-around bad boy from Toronto. I was smitten and charmed by his character. I later found out that he was a backslidden Christian. I couldn't believe it. How did he ever slip this far? I hadn't come across anyone who knew Jesus before and this just drew me closer to him. I had so many questions. Somehow, in my drug-induced illusions, I believed that God had sent T-Bone, as my knight in shining armour, to come and lead me to God. Perhaps, I thought, he would lead us both back to the Lord.

I had wanted God in my life, but I didn't feel worthy enough to attempt to go to Him. I was seeking answers from someone. I wanted someone to give me hope and to speak life into me. I thought maybe this man would be the one. I couldn't have been more wrong. Instead, it was this friend, who had once been a born-again Christian, who introduced me to crack cocaine. One day while we were at home, I walked into the room while he was putting something away. It was his crack pipe.

I found out T-Bone not only believed in God, but had also been a Spirit-filled believer. I wanted to know more about God, but T-Bone never wanted to talk about it. He stayed away from the subject and it always left me wondering. Whenever I walked on the block now, things seemed different. I knew there was much more to life than this. The hustlers were always moving and the girls in the alley were just trying to make enough money for their next fix. It left me wondering if this was it for my life.

Was I going to die like this? Would I ever escape this? Was this how it was going to end? Smoking a crack pipe?

We lived in the east end of London for a short while, until things between Dee and I soured and we started to have some major blow ups. It erupted to a point where one night T-Bone and I were out of the apartment and on the block, living from one motel to the next. As our drug use progressed, I was becoming invisible, merely existing.

One Christmas morning as I headed over to our motel room riding the city transit, I fell asleep. I remember being awakened by a police officer as he was hovering over me, asking me if I was ok. I was so humiliated. The bus driver said I had been driving with him for sometime. It concerned him that

I never got off the bus. He said he tried repeatedly to wake me up, but couldn't. I got up and, with my head hanging down, took off as fast as I could. Oh my goodness! I couldn't believe I fell asleep on the city bus.

Life for me regressed downhill. I often wondered if I would get out of what seemed to be hell. I remember "jonesing," going through withdrawal, combing the floors on my hands and knees in my motel room looking for any piece of crack I could find. But all I found was dirt and bread crumbs. I can remember days watching the Christian TV station and hearing the message about God. All I could think was that this message was for someone else who hadn't yet screwed up their life – I was too far beyond help.

One evening while T- Bone was out hustling, he made a contact and we were going to meet him later that night. When we met him I couldn't help thinking that this man seemed very familiar to me. But I didn't remember from where? A while later, while we were smoking crack with him, I remembered. This man used to go to the same church I attended when I was younger. I couldn't believe it!

There was no way this could be the same man, I thought. I remember back in church, this man worshipped and loved the Lord and now he too was out here! God, what was happening? My mother had told me that something had happened at church and the pastor stepped down. Our pastor had made advances toward a lady from our congregation.

Was this man's turning from the Lord the result of a pastor who failed? I wasn't sure, but I was deeply saddened by this. Where we once stood together and sang songs of worship, now we were sitting together getting high. Oh Lord, be merciful and help us. How does it happen? Why do some men of God proclaim to know God and yet live contrary to the Word of God? I didn't get an answer, but it was a question I held close to my heart.

As our drug use progressed, T-Bone and I had to find alternate ways to pull in money. We started to boost — to steal — high-quality clothes in large quantities from different department stores. We would walk in with a duffel bag in tow and T-Bone would have me be the look-out. He would then quickly grab a bundle from the rack and fill his bag. We did this in exchange for our drugs. They took the clothing and sent it out to wherever. We didn't care. We just wanted one thing.

Then one day, as we were leaving a store with our duffel bag full, security grabbed me. We had almost made it out the door. T- Bone took off out the doors and I tried squirming free but to no avail. I was quickly brought down to the floor. T-Bone was shortly apprehended in the parking lot. I remember riding up the escalator with security and feeling so humiliated, but I didn't say a thing, I just hung my head. T-Bone claimed it was him who they wanted and he ended up with a few months in secure custody. I had no other charges and so my charges were dropped.

There was another girl I knew on the block whose name was also Sonia. She was also a native girl. One morning they found her body on the outskirts of London. She had been beaten to death. She was found only with a pair of socks on. Some thought this was me. Some even looked disappointed it wasn't me. It was hard to believe that she was here only a moment ago and now she was gone. Was I afraid to die? Yes. I was and I didn't want to end my life like this. I wanted a better life. I just didn't know how to do that. I had already had some bad dealings and scary encounters which could have easily taken my life.

People looking to get high only care for one thing – getting high. Things were changing and they were ending. T-Bone was becoming more and more abusive. Smoking the narcotics made him paranoid. Doors and windows needed to be closed. This only intensified my own fears. We were staying in a motel in the south end of London and running out of options. It was becoming harder and harder to function properly. The withdrawals and constant feeding of the addiction was becoming impossible to afford. We couldn't afford our room. We were forced to hustle from hour to hour.

It felt like death was at the door and I was scared. I didn't know what was going to happen. T-Bone would talk about God, and then we would both feel worse. We knew that soon we would both be feeling the depths of hell if something didn't change. Then finally, T-Bone called his former pastor for help. He told his pastor about me and his pastor wanted me to go to drug rehab. I decided to go. He came to pick me up and I left T-Bone for the last time. He was heading back to Toronto.

~nine~

Maybe God Still Loved Me

Isaiah 59:1
Behold, the LORD's hand is not shortened, that it cannot save; neither his ear heavy, that it cannot hear:

The drug rehab center was located just outside of Kingston Ontario. The trip was over before I could remember. All I could recall was how fast we were travelling. Everything was just a blur. We arrived and I don't even recall saying thank you or good-bye to the Pastor who had taken time to drive me to this center. I just grabbed my bags and went directly into the center.

Once I was admitted the staff confiscated my bags and began a search of my things looking for drugs or anything they deemed inappropriate. When they finished, I wasn't allowed to have anything or wear any of my clothing – it was all inappropriate. At that moment, I decided I was going to hit the road. I wasn't going to stay. I was going to get out of there. I could feel the stares from the other girls and my walls of bitterness and hatred flared up. I wanted to sucker punch some of them!

The next day, my intent to escape was still strong. To my luck, we were allowed outside. As everyone was busy I made my escape. I hitched a ride into Kingston and when I arrived in town, I called a guy I had met days before from London. His name was Amid and he was from the Middle East. He paid my bus ticket to head back to London. Once back in London I stayed with him. I had nothing, except the clothes on my back.

This marked the beginning of another relationship. I still wanted to party, but as time passed I gradually began to fall for this man. He bought me nice things and spoiled me. I knew this man genuinely cared for me and I slowly began to pull back from the bar scene and commit myself more to this relationship.

One night, while I was out partying, I ended up over at a friend's house wanting and hoping to party some more. Samantha was just like me. She loved to party. We only had a few drinks, but now we wanted something more than a drink. We both needed a fix. The problem was that neither of us had money and she had nothing to front or bargain with. She made phone call after phone call trying to make a drug score, but nothing looked promising. There were a couple of calls that we had hoped would produce a score. All we could do was wait for one of her contacts to call back. (My drug use was becoming less often now, but whenever I drank, I could smell and taste the cocaine. I could never be sure where I would end up.)

It got quiet as we sat there and waited. Then, without saying a word, Samantha turned off the kitchen light. The only light that came through was from the street light outside. It was then that I felt things get very eerie. As I sat there, watching her, I saw the knife. From where I was sitting it looked like she got it from underneath her chair. I felt like I was watching something from a horror movie. I wasn't. This was real life. And this was a real knife. I asked her what she was doing and she turned towards me and told me to shut my mouth. She was not a small girl. She was larger than I was in stature. We had been in a physical altercation once before, but we had managed to make up. I knew she was a dirty fighter. With a knife in her hand, I wasn't going to risk a fight. She was serious. She pointed it towards me and threatened to cut my eyes out. I wasn't allowed to move or talk.

Moments later, there was a knock on the door. Samantha had left the door unlocked. This poor girl, who was totally unaware of what was happening, walked in. Once she was inside we were both told to shut up and stay seated. I sat there and couldn't believe that this was happening. Had my friend totally lost it? We sat there in silence. Samantha had complete control. Her knife made sure of that.

Some time passed and I told Samantha I needed a drink of water. She agreed. As I headed to the kitchen, I tripped over the phone cord and the phone crashed to the floor. She got up and started screaming and yelling. As she came over to pick up the phone, she laid her knife on the table. I saw my window of opportunity. With only seconds to move, I grabbed the beer bottle that was in front of me and smashed it over her head. Quickly, while she struggled to regain herself, I grabbed the knife. The other girl and I both made a run for it. Like a slow motion scene from a horror movie, I looked back and saw her rising up to come after me. I held the knife in my hand facing toward her and hoped this mad woman wouldn't lunge at me. Though I was hurt and confused by what had happened, Samantha was still my friend.

With her still coming after me I backed out of her townhouse rear entrance and made it outside. As soon as I was outside I ran to any nearby door I could find. Still holding the knife, I knocked on the door. A woman answered and once she did I collapsed onto her steps and broke down. As I sat there on those steps I wondered what was going to happen to my friend and her daughter. She had a beautiful daughter who had been upstairs during this entire episode. I learned later on that Samantha had taken off and had tried to hide out. A short time later she returned home and was apprehended.

A few years later, I saw her picture on the local news station. She had been mistakenly released from jail and the public was informed she was not to be approached. She had been doing time for allegedly stabbing someone. Where she had failed with me she had been successful in stabbing someone else. I don't know what happened to Samantha. I may not ever know why she pulled a knife on me that night. Regardless, I love her, and she is in my prayers. This was one of the last few times I would relapse.

My relationship with Amid continued. At different times our relationship would almost end. We were two people with two different types of addictions. But both were bad. Amid loved to gamble and I loved to drink. Together, we were not a good combination. Then, when everything was almost out of control, I found out I was pregnant. When this news settled, we were happy. Or at least we thought we were. We were both under this illusion that a child would somehow make everything better for us. I was overjoyed with having a baby and so was he. It didn't change our inner battles however. We started talking about marriage, thinking that this was what we needed to do for our child. But things just became worse between him and I. We were fighting all the time and he continued his gambling addiction. I would scream and fight all the time with him. It was horrible, but it was just more evidence of the cycle of abuse I found myself caught in. Good days would only be met with worse days. The only thing that had changed was time.

In October 1995, our son, Hassan Crane, was born. He was the cutest thing that hit the planet. My goodness! He was so adorable and I loved him dearly. When our boy was three months old, Amid decided to go to the Middle East to visit his family. I was crushed and terribly hurt.

I decided to leave and go to western Canada. Saskatchewan was my home province and it was time for our son to get to know my family. My mother was still living her party lifestyle and knowing this made me feel very alone and scared. I kept a journal and would write whatever was on my heart. Although I didn't pray much, I wrote what I felt. I asked the Lord to help me raise my child. I asked Him to lead me and direct me. I asked Him to give me wisdom, and I asked Him to forgive me.

I poured my heart out on those pages. And I know without a doubt today that the Lord heard every whimper and every cry from my heart. He was going to do great things for us. "Help me raise this son You gave me because I don't know what I'm doing."

I often thought about my experience at camp as a child. Maybe I could return to the Lord. Maybe He still loved me.

Leaving for western Canada seemed like the best thing to do. It was time to get to know my family. I had been gone a long time and really hadn't stayed in touch with family, except of course *Kokum* and a couple of close cousins. I was excited to be near *Kokum* again. I sincerely hoped that everything would fall into place now. It was time for my boy and me to get to know our family. This time was way past due. And perhaps, just maybe, I would have the answers I needed to hear from my dad. Many of the family members on my dad's side were Christians and involved in ministry. I thought that maybe, possibly, they could help lead me in the Lord's direction, because I was in dire need of it.

We left after Amid left for the Middle East. Our trip west was both exciting and terrifying because I decided to take the plane. I hated flying, but with my young baby, it seemed easier. We arrived alive and our first stop was at my dad's house. My dad had been on the road and hadn't arrived home yet. I had hoped that this visit would be enjoyable. As I waited for my dad to arrive, his wife and I began small talk to pass the time. Soon however, we exchanged some choice words with each other. Upset, I called my cousin who lived in Saskatoon, Saskatchewan, and told her what had happened. She invited us to come to her place. I packed up and left.

So now, we were on our way to Saskatoon. I fell in love with the city. It was beautiful. This was where I decided to make our home. We moved into a three-story walk-up apartment which was close to my aunt's house. They lived only a few blocks away and I was happy. They were ministers of the gospel. They traveled in ministry and held church meetings in their basement. Things were changing and looking better and I decided to have my son dedicated to the Lord.

I was happy to be closer to *Kokum* but she was still three hours away. I know she was happy too that we were closer now. She fixed up her little 1989 Nissan car for me. She was going to help us out however she could. I can remember even as a teenager, she tried to have me come back to Saskatchewan to be close to her, but by that time I was already too ashamed. I had already done so many things I didn't want her to know about. Staying away was easier and I could hide my failures. Now I was here and if things came up with *Kokum*, I would have to be honest. That was one of my prayers to the Lord that I wouldn't ever bring shame to *Kokum*. Somehow, someway, she wouldn't have to know the details.

Within six months, I started to get lonely. I missed London. The happy reunion I had envisioned with my dad never happened. Although we talked on the phone occasionally, it wasn't the same. He never once came to see me.

It was so disheartening. I just wanted to leave. I was thankful for *Kokum*, my aunt, my cousin and her husband. Even now, I can't thank them enough for all their hospitality. Yet with all their kindness and goodness toward me, I was missing my home. I was missing London, Ontario.

It was extremely hard to break the news to *Kokum*. When I did, I knew she was very upset with me. She was visibly shaken and saddened. It would be hard for her to be without me again. Having broke the news to her brought some finality to my decision. It was settled. I was leaving. I was heading back to eastern Canada. I was heading back to London.

I decided that it was best if I just got rid of all my belongings. I tried to reach my dad before leaving, but he didn't return my phone call. I was left feeling angry and bitter. I just couldn't understand. I had so many questions and so many of those questions were going to be left unanswered.

One day I received a call. It was from a Christian woman that lived over in the next building. We'd had coffee before and I knew she loved the Lord; she always carried a Bible with her. She told me that she was just about to head out the door when the Lord had given her a word for me. I didn't know what to say, but I was definitely moved. No one had ever spoken a word to me before like this.

Romans 8:18 NKJV
For I consider that the sufferings of this present time are not worthy to be compared to the glory which shall be revealed in us.

I didn't understand exactly what this scripture meant. All I knew was that I was given some kind of a promise. Nothing made sense to me. All I had were more questions, "*Why wasn't anything working out? Why was this happening to me?*"

I met Amid in London and we continued living together for another two years. When things finally ended we had been living in Calgary, Alberta. We had gone out to western Canada because he was able to find a lot of work there. But everything came to a halt one night and it was over. I packed up my suitcase and left. With my bag in one hand and my young son in the other we boarded a bus. We were bound back to Ontario. We were bound for London. We arrived and, until I could find my own place, we stayed at my mother's house. It was time to start over again.

~ten~

You're Only Passing Through

Micah 7:15
According to the days of thy coming out of the land of Egypt will I shew unto him marvellous things.

My mother was still doing a lot of partying and within a short time, I started partying as well. I started going out to the clubs and drinking – a lot! One night, while mom was partying at home and blasting the music, I went upstairs to check up on Hassan. I managed to slip in without waking him. I laid down beside him and watched my precious child sleep. An overwhelming love for him filled me. Tears began rolling down my cheeks while shame, guilt, and failure taunted me. Dread filled my heart of what I was doing to my baby. Feeling sick and hung over made it even worse.

Mesmerized by his beautiful angelic little hands and feet, I realized that this life before me was a miracle. God had given me this beautiful child and here I was failing at being his mother. I was giving my boy the same life I endured, and my heart broke for him and everything I had become. This heaviness seemed to become even heavier. Feeling so alone, thoughts of suicide ran rampant through my mind. I hated myself. My son, who had been given to me, deserved so much more. Why had he been given to me? My heart was seared with pain thinking about my son's future.

I couldn't take it anymore. I wanted to die. I wanted all this pain to go away. In the midst of this turmoil, I heard His voice. I heard the audible voice of the Lord. He said to me, *"You're only passing through."* Tears began streaming down my face. His presence was so near. In that instant, I knew everything was going to be ok.

I knew I was in the Lord's hands. I'm not sure what I was expecting to happen because I didn't know. Deep within, I knew the Lord was with me. Yet, the things in my life grew progressively worse. I continued partying. Nothing changed and everything seemed the same as before. One thing I knew for certain was that I didn't like being alone. I hated being alone. It was too much for me to be alone. My thoughts would overwhelm me.

It was then that I met Khalil who was also from the Middle East. Weeks into our relationship, an acquaintance of his told me to be careful. I didn't heed his warnings. Instead I continued to fall in love, or at least what I thought was love. Khalil seemed nice enough, but it was only a matter of weeks before I understood his friend's warning.

Khalil became extremely jealous and possessive. Although I knew this relationship wasn't going to go anywhere, I continued to see him. We had always lived apart which, I believe, kept us both sane. Somehow, in my mind, I believed we could change each other. As time passed, I just started to accept the bad treatment that I got. As much as we wanted change, and as much as we wanted it to get better, things got worse. It was an impossible situation. What alarmed me the most about this situation was the degree to which we will lower ourselves so that we don't have to be alone. Now, instead of one unhappy cookie we had two unhappy cookies. And neither was really worth the bite.

Khalil was a gambler. I didn't mind because when we went to the casinos, I did my drinking. The trip home was always the worst. With the amount of money that he would lose he would end up broke and close to crying. I didn't help matters. Being drunk, all I wanted to do was argue or fight. It was just bad.

Hassan's father, Amid, was back in the province and we started court proceedings for custody. The court awarded me sole custody and child support. Amid was given access to Hassan every other weekend. This gave me my weekends free to go out. It wasn't before long that I was going out every weekend.

It was around this time that I had a dream that shook me. I dreamt that I had been arrested. I was being taken up a long spiral flight of stairs and I remember having an awful feeling in my stomach that I was going to jail for a very long time. The fear I felt was so real and I remember screaming and crying, "I'm never going to see my son again!" Thankfully, it was just a dream and I woke up. That dream scared me to the realization that this would and could happen to me. I would go out drinking and would not know when to quit. I was always fighting. I know this dream was from the Lord. It was His warning to me.

One incident in particular took place in 1998. Hassan's dad was bringing him home on a Sunday after having his weekend visit. When he brought Hassan in to the house, Amid found me passed out on the couch. This infuriated him and he contacted the authorities. I was physically shaken at the prospect of losing my son. Although the authorities did not feel a need to open a case for this because my son had not been in my care at that time, it was a blow that helped me look at my life. It woke me up and made me realize what my son was enduring at my hands. I had so many friends already who had had their children apprehended because of abuse or no food in the house. More alarming was that some just didn't want their children – they wanted to party. This wasn't my heart; I wanted to be a good mother. I wanted to raise my son and see him thrive in life. My biggest worry was raising him to be like me. I knew what I wanted but how was I going to get us there. Anyone familiar with addictions knows what I mean. I wanted and desired the best and would tell myself "*This will be my last drink,*" or "*This will be my last time going out.*" Even with the hangover, the guilt, and remorse, it never is the last time. After just a few days the feelings of remorse were gone. And so was I!

Little did I know that my life would soon take another turn.

It was the summer of August 1999 and we were now living in the west end of London. My son was at his dad's for the weekend so as usual I decided to go out. I went to a local pub downtown I frequently visited.

During the night, a sister of a native woman I knew was there and I could feel her staring at me. I knew I wasn't on her list of favourite people. She came up to me and we exchanged some heated words. Before I knew it she had pushed me backwards. Instinctively, I struck back hitting her in the face. The owner came to ask her to leave and she yelled at me to follow her outside to finish what was started. I was about to follow her when the friends I was sitting with told me to forget about her and enjoy the rest of the evening. This idea sounded better, so I stayed.

I ended up staying until closing time and then went home. Once home I went to the kitchen to cook myself something to eat. Not long after, I heard my name being called in the building. I recognized the voice; it was the sister of the woman I had had the altercation with at the pub that night. Obviously, she had gone home and convinced her sister that together they should pay me a visit. I could hear them knocking on my neighbours door down below and I could hear them calling my name. They were waking up the building and so I knew I had to go down and see them. I wasn't going to back down from anyone. My alcohol-induced state only made me rashly, and irrationally, braver. Before going down, just to be safe, I looked out my apartment window and saw a cab in the parking lot. This gave me some assurance that things would be ok. I didn't want them coming around when my son was home.

When I got downstairs, I met them in front of the building. Before I even knew what was happening they were both hitting me. They knocked me to the ground and continued beating me. Over and over they kicked my head and body, until I couldn't feel anything anymore. I heard a man yelling "Stop, you're going to kill her!" They took off and the next thing I remembered was him carrying me inside the building to a downstairs apartment. Once inside, the police were called.

When the police arrived, they informed me that they had apprehended the women just down the street and that they were pressing charges. They wanted to take me to the hospital but I refused to go. That's when the constable told me to go and look in a mirror. I couldn't believe what I saw! All I could do was cry. I was no longer recognizable. My face was swollen and was black and blue beyond recognition. I suddenly became afraid fearing any internal injuries. I knew full well that the alcohol I had consumed numbed any pain. Heeding the constable's instruction, I went to the hospital.

Once I arrived at the hospital they ran some tests and asked if I could be pregnant. I didn't think so, but I wasn't on any birth control. They ran the test and it was that night I found out I was two months pregnant.

Khalil arrived at the hospital to see me and he couldn't believe what had happened. But he was quite happy to hear I was pregnant. With the state my life was in the news of a baby frightened me.

How was I going to raise two babies?

My son's dad came to see me and he was very upset by what happened. He got so angry. When I saw my son, shame filled my heart. I couldn't tell him that his mother had been out drinking and had been fighting. So instead, I told him I fell down the stairs.

What else could I say?

The headaches that followed were excruciating. Hassan's school was a few blocks away and walking him was a painful ordeal. Every step I took hurt. And now there was a baby forming inside me.

Yes, I was scared and I remember feeling so alone. All I could think was 'another child?'

I had always dreamed of having many children. I loved little babies and had always wanted a big family, a nice house, and a white picket fence. I tried to be a good mom and I loved my son dearly. He was a gift from the Lord.

My guilt of not being a better mom and not being able to give him more was destroying me. The thought of another child was weighing me down even further. To have a baby from the man I wanted to get away from depressed me more.

Even after the vicious attack I had received I continued my drinking. I would often visit the illegal after-hours clubs. I knew my assailants would be there. I didn't care. Nothing was going to deter me from drinking. My drinking and smoking would continue well into my sixth month of pregnancy. The drinking finally slowed down somewhat after the sixth month, but I still went out on occasion. It didn't help that during this time the fighting with Khalil intensified.

I started to feel more and more movement from within, and I could feel the baby rolling and jumping around. I wanted this life and I was going to love her. Although I hadn't been told the gender of my baby, I knew I was having a girl. I was still very scared but I knew I had to try harder to turn my life around. I would watch my son play and soon my hidden cries were becoming vocal. I was crying out unto the Lord more often.

Khalil and his jealous obsessions with me intensified. He wanted to know every move I made and even where I went. I was now carrying his child and, in his mind, this gave him ownership over me. Khalil would come to my apartment anytime he wanted and all this was making me nervous. I thought of my son, Hassan, and how it would affect him if he saw me being hit. I knew I couldn't allow that. I knew what it was like when you watch someone you love get hurt and the helplessness you feel. I can remember shaking with convulsions as a little girl while I watched the one I loved get thrown around and beaten.

I knew it was time to get away from this man, but how? How were things going to get better? How was I going to break out of this cycle?

During my pregnancy, I decided that I was going to name my baby Hasslina. This infuriated Khalil. He wanted a son. Even mentioning a girl bothered him and made him angry. It didn't matter; my love for my girl was growing. With each passing day drawing nearer to my delivery date, I knew I had to leave. Heaviness and dark clouds seemed to follow me everywhere. And it made me afraid. I felt imprisoned and trapped. This prison I was in was real. I felt shackled and chained. I knew my only answer was God. I had heard of bondage before and I knew my children and I needed help. I knew I was in a spiritual bondage. I just knew I had to get away from Khalil. Maybe being out of the city would do just that. St. Thomas was a small town twenty minutes south of

London. It seemed to be the perfect place for us. It was far enough away from Khalil, but close enough for him to see his daughter.

I began praying daily, "*Lord, if you help me find a place with a church, school, and a store within walking distance, I'll move there, just help me!*" I was at the end of myself, my baby was going to be born soon, and I just needed to find shelter for us. I was already a little more than six months pregnant by then. Khalil said that he would drive me there to go look at some places and I was happy.

The first house I looked at wasn't much but I saw it as my escape and I took it. I took it because it had all the three things I had asked of the Lord and I knew things would be ok. All three things were within a three block radius of one another. I paid the rent and the deposit and it was mine. The Lord's hand was in this and it was going to be our home. Khalil was happy about this too, in fact, it was perfect for him, and I was out of sight. His possessiveness and jealousy still made me uneasy. I was just happy to be farther away from him and now I could focus on getting my life right.

Down the street was a Pentecostal church and I started attending. Little by little, it seemed, we were making progress. St. Thomas didn't have much of a bus system, so I still had to depend on Khalil. He would take me shopping whenever he came to visit. We were still seeing each other, but I hated it.

When was I ever going to be free from him?

The likelihood of this happening seemed unlikely now since I was going to have his child. I knew my children and I deserved more. But I just didn't know how to do it. How was I finally going to break away? After three months in that place, the Lord moved us into a nicer and bigger place.

~eleven~

Turning Away From the Snares of Death

Luke 13:12
And when Jesus saw her, he called her to him, and said unto her, Woman, thou art loosed...

March 16, 2000

My baby's birth day was here, and I was so grateful to have my mom with me. I had started to get mild contractions early in the morning. The contractions were beginning to come more frequently and I knew it was time to wake up my mom. At around 6:00 a.m., my contractions were coming fast and it was time to go to the hospital. I called Khalil and told him it was time. By the time we arrived at the hospital, I was bending over with each contraction. After they admitted me, I had to change into my hospital gear, and with each contraction, the pain was becoming more and more unbearable. There were a few times I wanted to punch Khalil because, with each contraction I had, he laughed. This was his first baby. We had not gone to any prenatal classes together so he didn't know what to expect. I knew he was very nervous and excited.

The doctor finally arrived at around 8:00 a.m., and I was amazed by his calmness. He came in to the labour room cool, calm, and collected. He looked at his watch and informed me that my baby would be born at noon. Sure enough, my baby girl arrived right at 12:00 p.m. When the doctor announced she was a girl, Khalil looked upset for a brief moment, until he heard her cry, and this broke his heart. I could see the love for her in his eyes. I could see that he was smitten by her.

When it came time to cut the umbilical cord, the doctor handed the scissors to Khalil. I thought he was going to pass out. A look of fear crossed his face and he quickly shook his head, "No." I guess I should have explained to him what was going to happen. I still tease him about it and we can laugh about it now. Then the doctor handed the scissors over to my mom. She had no problem with cutting the umbilical cord. After a quick snip, my girl was handed over to me. I was in awe of her beauty. She was all that I could have hoped for. She was perfect. When I counted her toes I saw five perfect baby toes with an extra cute toe on each end. Twelve toes! We were blessed.

I named her Hasslina Joy after my mom. Our local paper, the London Free Press, gave an update of my progress of having given birth to a healthy baby girl despite the beating I had endured.

We were discharged from the hospital on schedule. I was so thankful for this because Hassan had been admitted for a few days after birth because of jaundice. Hasslina was healthy and bright pink! We were able to take her home and Hassan was excited at now having a sister. With a small family, I had high hopes for the future. What should have been a great beginning only became worse for us.

Khalil and I argued all the time. He would be infuriated if I didn't let him come over when he wanted to. He threatened to kidnap our daughter, leave the country with her, and that I would never see her again. As scary as he had made it for me, I pursued custody through the courts and filed for child support. Although it was a gruelling and stressful time, it drew me closer to the presence of the Lord. I continued to cry unto the Lord to help us and save us. I didn't want this way of life anymore.

In 2001, I received sole custody and child support for my girl, Hasslina Joy Crane.

Things stayed the same for a while. I continued to see Khalil. I called the police a few times but nothing much ever came of it. It seems a few days would pass and I would let him come back. We would both say all the right things, and make the right promises to each other, but things never got better. It was our hearts that were sick. All we were to one another was the other's crutch. More and more my eyes were being opened.

"Lord, I don't know how I'm going to make it with two kids on my own. My babies won't have

their father." I knew first-hand what it was like to be without a father and now my babies would have to live without theirs. "God help us...Lord help me to break away from this relationship. Lord, help us."

The more I began to pray and draw closer to the Lord, the more I began feeling the Lord's conviction in my heart. Whenever the Word of God would be brought forth I began to understand and see the cost of my fornication with Khalil. I didn't want to feel this way anymore. I didn't want to be used anymore. The sexual bond between us needed to be broken. The union of marriage was created for a man and woman and this is what pleased the Lord. I was living in fornication and I needed to make a choice. Although I longed for marriage, I knew this wasn't it.

Proverbs 14:27 NKJV
The fear of the Lord is a fountain of life, to turn one away from the snares of death.

There was a reverence and fear in my heart for God. As I was drawing in closer to Him, I knew He required obedience. There were greater things and a deeper walk than what I already knew. I needed to make a choice and stick to it; this relationship was going to destroy my children and me.

It was then that I opened my heart and shared all my fears with the Lord. I began asking Him for strength so I could stand up to Khalil. I didn't like my life anymore and didn't want it anymore. It was empty. This life I had in Christ, meant more to me than anything else I knew. It was a constant battle and the more I pressed in closer to Him, it seemed the more I slipped up. Whenever I would slip up with Khalil, I would be beaten down by condemnation the following day.

What was wrong with me? Why couldn't I obey? For days after I would search my heart and ask, 'Is it worth it for me to lose my salvation for this? Or to lose the salvation of my children? Am I going to risk eternity for a moment of pleasure?' No, I didn't want to. It wasn't worth it. I just hoped that the Lord would not turn away from me.

It all hit me like a ton of bricks one evening. That morning Khalil had left after spending the night. Feelings of shame and guilt flooded my heart and all I could do was weep. I felt like the woman who had been caught in adultery. In times past she would have been put to death by stoning, and I felt that I deserved the same sentence. I felt so ashamed and deserving of those stones. The condemnation was overwhelming. Soon accusing voices would cry out in my ears that I would never be enough, and that I could never change. Sadly, I accepted them. I came to a decision that I would never be able to change. I backed away from Christ. I didn't want to hear Christian music anymore and I wasn't going to think about Him.

It was only a few hours later, after these accusing voices had left, that the Lord stirred my heart. He never threw any stones at me, but told me He loved me, and always did. His grace was here and His grace was more than sufficient to help and nurture me until I grew.

> **2 Corinthians 12:9 NKJV**
> **"My grace is sufficient for you, for My strength is made perfect in weakness," Therefore most gladly I will rather boast in my infirmities, that the power of Christ may rest upon me.**

Although we may fail, His grace is there. Where sin abounded, grace abounded much more (Romans 5:20). When we come to Christ, we are babes in Him, and He is patient until we receive strength and understanding in His Word. Christ is here to walk with us all the way. As long as we walk toward Him and press into Him, He is going to be there to pick us up. We must turn to the Lord continually; He is our way, our truth, and our life. His way to us is through our hearts so that He may win our hearts.

As I became more serious, and God's strength grew in my life to let go of my relationship with Khalil, our arguments intensified. He threatened to take the lives of my children, his own, and mine. The threats that came never bothered me that much; I knew the Lord would protect us.

There was one night when Khalil pleaded with me to come over to my house, but I would not budge. I continued to refuse until he blew up and began threatening me. Somewhere in the midst of our conversation, I quoted the scripture, "No weapon formed against me shall prosper." I know he must have thought I was crazy. He told me, "If I put a gun to your head and pulled the trigger it's going to kill you." Of course, I knew this to be true, but in my heart I knew it wasn't going to happen. Later, he told me that it was always the half hour drive that would calm him down, and he would turn around and go back. The Lord was changing his heart and I knew the Lord had His hand on me. It was His hand that intervened to move me and save me. My stay in St. Thomas was a turning point in our lives that I will never forget.

~twelve~

Freedom!

Psalm 37:23
The steps of a good man are ordered by the Lord and He delights in his way.

I continued to grow daily in the things of the Lord by reading His Word. This is what Khalil didn't know. I was reading the Word diligently and my confidence in Christ continued to grow. I had Christ in me. I was not standing alone anymore.

> **1 John 4:4 NKJV**
> **You are of God little children, and have overcome them, because He who is in you is greater then he who is in the world.**

I began writing my Bible scriptures on cue cards to memorize them. I knew that these words were going to change my life forever. More and more I began to understand the words that the Lord had spoken to me, "You're only passing through." Yes, this place is only temporary. I was finally at the end of myself and realized the Lord was everything I needed. Christ was the only one who could heal my broken heart and restore my family, but it was going to come one day at a time.

I was so moved by the story of this woman, in the book of Luke, who had been down and tormented for so long. It moved me to tears.

> **Luke 13:11-13 NKJV**
> **And behold, there was a woman who had a spirit of infirmity eighteen years, and was bent over and could in no way raise herself up. But when Jesus saw her, He called her to Him and said to her, "Woman, you are loosed from your infirmity." And He laid His hands on her, and immediately she was made straight, and glorified God.**

She was cast down and couldn't even raise her head. I thought Luke was talking about me! And of course *he was talking about me!* And I'm sure he is talking about many others who are in the same situation. You're cast down and in distress. You are so burdened down with guilt and shame that it's hard to raise your head. You are full of torment and have no peace. You feel sick in the mind and you ask yourself what can I do? I thank God for these stories. They're not just there to tell a good story, but they are there to edify and to lead us through.

1 Corinthians 10:11 NKJV
Now all these things happened to them as examples, and they were written for our admonition, upon whom the ends of the ages have come.

There is nothing new under the sun (Ecclesiastes 1:9) and the Lord knows of every detail of our lives. Though the enemy may come to growl and have us believe that we will never change, he is a liar and the father of it (John 8:44).

Christ, when He went to the cross, wiped out all the handwriting of requirements that was against us, which were contrary to us. He took it out of the way, having nailed it to the cross and having disarmed principalities and powers, He made a public spectacle of them, triumphing over them in it (Colossians 2:14-15).

I was loosed of my infirmities. I was free! I now had to learn to walk to become a soldier for the Lord Jesus, abounding in Him, that through Him others may be drawn in. Step by step, this little Indian girl was beginning to grow, and blossom into the woman of God whom Christ had called me to be. The Word of God was proving to be a lamp unto my feet and life with the Lord was good. It was all very exciting!

Everything in my life seemed to get better. The blackness and heaviness I had carried and that had followed me for many years was gone. I took driver training, and decided to get my license. This was a huge step for me; never did I think I would ever have my license, much less a car. My mom came out to baby-sit for me. Everything seemed to be going great. I was smiling more and for one reason only: *Christ Jesus was real and in my life!*

I became licensed and could now legally drive. I also wanted to go back to school, so I decided to move back to London. I knew it was time. My heart and mind were on the things of Christ now. My neighbours were also Christians and when I mentioned moving back to London, they said they would talk to their family who were landlords of a townhouse complex. I had been given favour. Once again, the Lord showed His love for me. He moved us into a beautiful complex in London. All the homes I had been moving into were subsidized and geared to my income. This was all so awesome.

Once we were finally settled, I enrolled in school and eventually bought my own car with help from my mom and Khalil. I loved going to the Christian bookstores and browsing through all the Christian music. They had so many Christian artists. I couldn't believe all the music they had. There were so many different genres. I especially loved the contemporary music and reggae. Wow, the Lord had so many called into the music ministry. I'd had no idea. I wanted to find testimonies so this was also the time I sought out books. I wanted to hear of others from my background for encouragement as my appetite for the things of God grew. I just wanted to read, and read it all.

During my search, I read some amazing stories of men and women of God. Their stories really touched my life and affected me greatly. They stayed faithful to the Lord because of their love for Him. During adversity and trials, Christ always helped them to overcome. This blessed my heart. I knew that one day I was going to share the things I had come through. Whenever I take a moment to reflect of where I came from, His love for me always amazes me.

Matthew 10:30
"But the very hairs of your head are all numbered."

My place was becoming a house of prayer and worship. I decorated my living room in scripture and I knew my friends thought I was losing my mind, but it didn't matter. Some of my friends have tattoos expressing who and what they believe in with symbols. They had all sorts of things hanging on their walls. And so I was going to openly express who I was, and who I was in love with. In large cursive handwriting on my wall, I painted "Jesus Lives!" It was my centerpiece. I was not ashamed. I was going to tell the world about Him and what He was doing. Like a newborn, I depended on the Father for His Word.

There was nothing in the world that I wanted anymore and nothing came remotely close to what I had now. The world and everything in it brought no satisfaction. The bars, the casinos, nice clothes, and playing dress up all had no allure to me anymore. Having a man on your arm who would buy you anything you desired was all a life without purpose. There was no foundation and no meaning in those things. There was more to life than dressing your life in goods and then to be put into a casket. All we have to do is look around to see there is something, someone, greater than us out there. I'm glad I found Him. If we were to be honest with ourselves we would see our desperate need for a Saviour.

I wasn't going to play charades or play with fire anymore. I was going to run with Jesus now. He was transforming me into something greater. Something far beyond any supermodel or anything else the world loves to idolize and be envious of. His greatness and His glory are so much more than we could ever imagine. I soon began to notice that everything in the world was growing dimmer, as the Lord grew brighter, and brighter, in my life.

> **Matthew 6:20 NKJV**
> **"But lay up for yourselves treasures in heaven, where neither moth nor rust destroys, and where thieves do not break in and steal:"**

What I had, no one could steal. And no one could separate me from my Father in Heaven (Romans 8:38-39). I was the King's daughter now and all was good. The knight in shining white armour I had yearned for had finally arrived. His name was Jesus!

I soon realized that being a King's daughter comes with responsibility. I was to be an ambassador of Christ's love. He was going to be bringing people into my life and I would have to learn to love them as He loved me. This life, I held within, was meant for others and I was about to be schooled. I remember one scripture I had been meditating on, it was;

> **Ephesians 4:29 NKJV**
> **Let no corrupt word proceed out of your mouth, but what is good for necessary edification, that it may impart grace unto the hearers.**

I decided to take the kids to the drive-in. After we got our popcorn and drinks and settled in for the movie, a car pulled up alongside ours. It was a woman and her boyfriend. Within a short time, they started arguing and cursing. I could tell this lady was obviously angry. Her language embarrassed me, but this was a mirror image of what I had sounded like whenever I got angry. I knew that the Word was a mirror to my own heart, and what I had seen in my heart was not good. The Lord, in His mercy and grace, was revealing the areas of my own heart that He wanted to cleanse and heal.

It was refreshing to see where I was going. Yet, at the same time, it was scary to see where I once was. I knew everything that came out of my mouth affected my children. I only wanted them to hear good things. This should extend to others around us as well. Christ is after our hearts. He desires to pour His love into our hearts so that we can share His love with others. The sharing of His desire with others can only be done in His love. Love is what men and women are searching for, and when they get weary of looking for it and not finding it, they begin to lose hope. Christ

Jesus came to give us hope, to give hope to people like you and me, so that we may become His.

~thirteen~

Restoring the Pieces

John 3:30

"He must increase, but I must decrease."

I ran into an old family friend named Abby. I hadn't seen her in years. Our reunion was a good one. The last time I saw Abby, she was just a little girl that used to scream and jump around a lot. She was the cutest little thing and now she was a young woman on fire for the Lord. Her mother and I had always been close and I guess this is why I was so drawn to her. I was just excited to finally meet up with her!

We had so much fun getting caught up and the Lord's timing was perfect because we both had a need at this time in our lives. I was enrolling in school and needed a babysitter and she needed a place. Everything fell together and she was so good with the kids, they loved her so much. She was such a blessing to our home.

After a few weeks of sharing living arrangements, things became a little more challenging. Living with someone can always get difficult and it was becoming a strain on both of us. I would get upset over something she did or didn't do, and so on. When you live with someone you see their habits and you become more aware of your own. I needed some serious changing in my own heart, and the closer that I drew into the presence of the Lord, the more I realized this.

Jeremiah 17:9
The heart is deceitful above all things, and desperately wicked; who can know it?

There were some hidden things in my heart and I knew what some of them were. They were wounds caused by rejection from my dad. Some were wounds caused by my mother. I needed healing.

Although many of these wounds had been caused as a child through actions of others, I didn't understand why they had been done. I was just a little girl who could not understand why the adults in my life had done the things they'd done. I knew I needed to forgive. But I had forgiven them, *hadn't I?* They were things of my heart that I really did not want to deal with.

Things between my mom and I were better, but I still found it difficult to talk with her. She still wasn't close to the kids and this hurt a lot.

One day she stopped in at my house and was only there for a few minutes. Just before she left, Hasslina noticed her and ran to put her shoes on. By this time, mom was already out the door and had left Hasslina at the screen door crying. This pierced my heart and made me so angry. I told Abby that I was seriously considering the idea of writing my mother a letter to sever ties with her forever, because I was so hurt. I knew my mother loved all of us, but it still hurt. Later that evening, Abby and I went before the Lord in prayer and asked him to soften my mother's heart. I wanted us to be a happy family and one that loved and stuck together.

I knew that the Lord had heard our prayers. The following day my mom came by again. This time, she asked to take the kids for a walk to the store. I said "Yes," of course, and off they went to the corner store. I looked at Abby and could feel tears well up in my eyes. "Thank-you Lord," I whispered, "for another answered prayer." The Lord was restoring our broken family. We had wanted to love and to be loved, but neither of us knew how to.

I knew our prayers had been heard. And gently, I could see that the love of God was beginning to pour and direct my mother and I back together. There was just so much hurt and anger in our hearts. Our lives weren't changed immediately, of course. We had to continually turn to the Lord and allow His Word to work through us. My mother was a big part of my life, and I longed for a relationship with her. And the Lord was giving that relationship back to us both. The Lord is good.

Even in the midst of this healing and restoration with my mom, I would still be stirred with emotions over the lost relationship with my father. I was at church service one morning when my heart was stirred for my dad. Tears began to well up in my eyes. I didn't want to cry. I fought back the tears. *"Lord not now," I pleaded.* I didn't want to cry and I didn't want to deal with this – not now! It was only a few years before that I recalled my aunt, on my dad's side, had called me with a question. She had asked me if I wanted any pictures of him. My cold response was "No!" In my heart I had thought that that part of my life was over. At least that is what I thought.

For many years, I had asked myself the question, 'Where was my dad?' 'Why didn't he phone and try to keep in contact with me over the years?' I wanted my dad. I had yearned for a relationship with him. But all I could think was what did I do or what didn't I do that kept him from me – his daughter? Where was he when I needed him? He was in ministry. He was supposed to minister hope to people, wasn't he? What about me? How were things going to change now? Isn't it too late now?

During the evenings, after the kids went down to sleep, Abby and I would make our tea and get comfortable in the living room. It was time to catch up on our missed years. Then it came. She started to ask questions about my dad. I really wasn't prepared for that. That was an area of my life I wanted to leave alone. I wanted to serve the Lord and leave my father out of this. I didn't want anything to do with my dad anymore. Having this sister in the Lord, asking me some things about my dad confirmed that the Lord wanted me to deal with this. I knew it was time to deal with the bitterness I was holding onto in my heart.

I told her that I had aunties and uncles, including my dad, who were involved in ministry. My dad was a preacher, an evangelist. I truly hoped that my bitterness wasn't being detected. For so long, I had asked the Lord so many questions myself and still didn't have any answers. Secretly, I hoped she wouldn't point out the obvious and ask about our relationship. I wasn't ready for the embarrassment. Thankfully, she never asked.

As we sat and talked, she read some scriptures from the book of Deuteronomy, explaining to me the favour of God in my life. In the passage, it spoke of possessing the land that was promised and given to our fathers. I understood this to mean that the Lord had given me favour because of the favour that he had bestowed upon my own father. I could not despise my dad without despising the favour of the Lord upon him. I knew the Lord was dealing with my heart. I needed to make things right with my dad, and with the Lord; *this meant total forgiveness*. It didn't matter if I thought my position was justified. I was commanded to forgive and love my father. I could not go on any further unless I obeyed. The inheritance of God that lay before me was mine if I wanted it. God was bringing me into a place where I would have to decide to obey Him and forgive, or walk in rebellion to His Word. I knew in my heart that if the Lord had brought me to this place then I would not disobey Him. I must forgive.

Once I made the decision to forgive my dad, the Lord in His faithfulness filled my heart with His love for him. It was then I felt the bitter waters leave. I knew I needed to call my dad's side of the family. The following night, I phoned a couple of my aunties and told them how much I loved them. I shared with them what the Lord was doing in my life. Despite the physical and emotional distance between us, God had fixed His eyes on me and always had.

A few weeks later, I was in my regular routine of boarding the city bus on my way to school. I boarded the bus and decided to grab a seat in the back. I plopped myself down in the seat and enjoyed the ride. As I sat there, staring out at the world through the window of the bus, I suddenly felt this great love and an overwhelming closeness for my dad. I then saw a vision of my dad and I sitting together having fellowship. I knew this was from the Lord. And I knew the time was coming soon that I would see my dad. I was overjoyed and so excited! It's difficult to explain how I felt about it all. All I knew at the time was that I just couldn't wait to tell Abby and my mom. I even called up my dad to let him know I was going to see him. I didn't know when, or how, but I was going to see him! I just couldn't wait for this to come to pass! Glory to God, I didn't have to wait long before my dad was sitting in my living room.

God worked things out incredibly. My aunt, who operates a Bible School in western Canada, takes her students to a camp in Deseronto, Ontario. It so happened that the Bible School needed a driver. Somehow, God worked it out that my dad was able to help. When he came, he stayed with us for about a week. I was just so happy to see him. We had lots of time to talk and hang out and just get to know each other. I was so thankful the Lord had prepared me for his coming, because I knew this was the start of a new beginning.

Joel 2:25
And I will restore to you the years that the locust hath eaten, the cankerworm, and the caterpillar, and the palmerworm, my great army which I sent among you.

We were all home visiting one evening when I went into the kitchen to do the dishes. I could see my dad from where I was standing. As I stood there watching him, I felt the familiar sting of rejection begin to rise; I called on the Lord.

I made a choice at that moment that I would not allow this to snare me again. This decision released an abundance of love for him. The choice had been mine to make. I could have taken hold of this familiar sting and embraced the bitterness, but I knew that it would only bring death. I was determined to hold on to the Lord's promise and what He had shown me as I rode the bus a few weeks before. I had to push aside every hindrance that came against me for this healing and relationship with my dad. God wanted us restored! And because I pressed through, God poured into me an all-consuming love for my father. From out of my heart flowed a love I had never experienced before for my dad. It was only a godly love that could have made this possible.

It was like seeing my dad for the first time. He was not on a pedestal – he was a man – and he was my father. He had his faults. He is, after all, human. As I allowed all my bitterness and anger to fall away, I could feel it as it was lifted from me. God in His mercy was ministering to my heart. Though I had been rejected, forgotten, and hopeless during the time on the street, the Lord was assuring me that He had been watching over me the whole time. He had heard my every cry. He had never forgotten me. The Lord was going to use me and I had to forgive and honour my father. We both needed to be restored to have the Lord's full blessing.

From that night on, my heart was filled with so much love for my dad. God had healed my heart that night, and still to this day He continues to bring my dad and I closer. I know my dad loved me and always did. Although there were different reasons for his absence in my life, despite what they were, I forgave him.

During his stay with us that week, my dad and I were browsing through the Internet. He took me to a website I had never heard of. It was David Wilkerson's website. I had no clue who this man was, and I had never heard of him before. But when I started to read about him and his amazing testimony,

I was blessed beyond measure. Here was a man of God! Because of his obedience thousands upon thousands had come to know the Lord. I became excited because the Word he preached confirmed so much in my heart. This was a man of truth! Here was a man who still preached on sin. Finding a man of God like this was, and is, becoming harder to find in this day and age. I was having such a hard time finding a home church because of this unwillingness by the carnal church to acknowledge sin. It seemed like everything that was coming from the pulpits were just empty messages. They had no power to change a person's life. There was no conviction. But now, I was able to receive some powerful life-changing messages online – *free of charge*! They were recorded at Times Square Church in New York City. I highly recommend this site for all who desire to hear a Word from the Lord. They preach the Word and without compromise. It will stir you and you will know it comes from the throne of God.

Although my dad had not been there for me physically, God was using my dad's hand to help feed me spiritually. I thank the Lord for my father, and for restoring us. The Lord's great faithfulness is beyond our human comprehension.

Ezekiel 36:26

A new heart also will I give you, and a new spirit will I put within you: and I will take away the stony heart out of your flesh, and I will give you an heart of flesh.

My heart, that was cold at one time, was becoming a heart of flesh. My heart was becoming soft and pliable and was being brought into a condition where God could work on it. Ever so slowly, and bit by bit, the Lord was changing me.

Abby and I grew in the Word by making each other accountable to memorize scripture. We loved the Word and ate it up. My house was covered and decorated in the Word. One evening as we sat and decorated more scriptures to hang up in the house, we decided to pray over them so whenever my brothers or visitors would come visit, it would minister to them. If the salvation of my brothers wouldn't come today or tomorrow it was going to come in an hour they least expected it.

The excitement of having scriptures decorating our home and being a witness to others birthed another idea. I wanted to provide multi-lingual scriptures to others. The idea sounded awesome! It had taken me weeks to provide an Arabic Bible to Khalil, so I knew that there was a real need for this. In most of the Christian bookstores I had been in, almost all of their publications were in English. That's when "G.O.D. Designs" was born.

It was during this time that the United States was embroiled in a bitter battle over the removal of the Lord's "Ten Commandments." Sadly, many were in favour of having them removed. A country that was born and blessed out of reverence and obedience to the Lord was now pushing the Lord out of every institution. It was both discouraging and encouraging to see that this anti-Christ spirit was rising – and is rising fast. It was discouraging to see how the Lord was being pushed out, and yet encouraging knowing that as this spirit of anti-Christ rises, it is only hastening the Lord's return. The time to work for the Lord was now. What had started as a passion for the Word had now birthed something in us that would provide others who shared our burden to reach the lost. G.O.D. Designs would be the voice to overcome the enemy who has tried to silence the Word. It would reach into places where we could not.

I started to remove things out of my house that were not pleasing to the Lord. I had many movies, and I got rid of them. Television was phased out of my home. I had no desire to watch it anymore. Whenever I would sit down to watch it, everything disturbed me. The language and sexual content of the commercials bothered me. I didn't see its purpose and I cut my cable. I was witnessing how subtle the enemy used this as an outlet to rob our families from spending time with the Lord. It's like food; whatever goes in must come out.

I wanted my children to conform to the things of the Lord, and not to the world. The violent video games and the horror movies we sat back and watched were making us cold and desensitized. As a nation we wonder why our children are suffering nightmares and becoming violent.

The different sitcoms I was watching started to bother me. Things that I once thought to be funny weren't funny anymore. If our adversary can keep us busy watching the sitcoms and soap operas instead of focusing on our own lives, he can subtly enter in and leave our lives in ruins while we sit around laughing at some senseless sitcom. Like a spy infiltrating our lives, the enemy slowly causes us to conform and model our lives after the lives of Hollywood celebrities. Yet, while we sit and watch their fake TV lives pass in front of us, many of them are succumbing to drug and alcohol addictions, broken marriages, and promiscuity. Even with all their fame, their money, and their million dollar mansions, they are not exempt from the enemy's attack to destroy their lives. Please do not misunderstand me; I am not suggesting that we all remove our televisions from our homes. Instead, with all things, we must use wisdom.

Serving the Lord was only becoming better and greater.

Things all around were getting better. My fears were leaving and my walk with the Lord intensified. The things I loved and wanted were now being put into proper perspective. I knew that Christ was going to walk me through more things that needed to be dealt with. My estranged relationship with my parents had been hindered because of sin, and we all suffered greatly because of it. We had lost our connection with one another and therefore it had made it so difficult for us to become connected later. It was only the love of our Heavenly Father that began to heal the wounds of the past. It was only Him that was joining us together once again.

Opening our hearts to the Lord in the prayer closet allows Him to work in us. With greater precision than any surgeon or doctor, Christ our Lord will explore our hearts to find and heal our most secret and deepest wounds. His ways are higher than ours. His desire in our lives is to make it so those wounds and sins we harboured will not be repeated in our children's lives. His eyes are on His children, and this includes yours and mine. Living as a single parent was challenging, and I know I could not have done it without the Lord. He had shown me how to love my kids and to become a better mom by staying connected with them. I was involved with my kids. I was spending time with them and listening to them. Whenever I was short with the kids, He would correct me and I would return to them with love. The Lord was showing me how to love and become a better mom. His provision and blessing in our lives have been great and He cares for the smallest areas of our lives.

I witnessed His faithfulness when my daughter had to undergo surgery for her feet. Hasslina had to have the extra small toes on her feet removed. Khalil and I were having a tough time with it. We didn't want to do it, but finding shoes for her was becoming a problem. My heart was so filled with worry, thinking about all the things that could go wrong. I remember being at the bus stop one day, filled with fear, when the Lord ministered to my heart. He assured me that all was going to be okay and that I needed to praise Him. He impressed upon me that I needed to praise

Him for the surgeons, to praise Him for all the good doctors, and for the care that she would receive. Everything was going to be ok. She belonged to the Lord. She had been given to me as a gift from the Lord, but He loved her more than I did. I had to trust Him.

Hasslina was almost two years old at the time. She would cry for me whenever we were in new surroundings. She didn't like me to leave her anywhere. This was one of my fears. I was afraid that she would be crying and screaming for me when they took her in. On the morning of her surgery while we waited, she seemed so content. She had been changed and was ready for surgery and she stayed seated in her large caged crib. I think the crib frightened me more than anything else. She didn't cry, not even a whimper. I was in awe of what I was witnessing and how much the Lord cared for every part of my life.

As I was witnessing the healing that was taking place in my heart with my mother and father, I was excited for what lay ahead. In all the time that I had been doing things my way and allowing my heart to become cold and hardened, I had lost the most important relationships to me. If it hadn't been for the Lord, I would have been well on my way to losing my children too. Lies and more lies from the pit of hell had me believe and see only the worst in everybody. The adversary wanted to destroy my life, and every good thing the Lord had planned for it.

Then something happened I did not expect. His light soon exposed something I held within my heart since I was a child that needed healing. It stemmed from an intrusion that had tried to take my life – twice – when I was still a small girl. Assaults that been done toward me. Sexual assaults. They had left me feeling marked and dirty. It was a perversion that I had prayed would never come near my dwelling again.

That evening as I lay on my bed reading a book, it felt like hands were literally lifted from my body. It was the hands of my abusers being lifted from me. Though their physical touch could harm me no more, it was the memory of their heavy breathing and the images that haunted me. But that night, God did something for me that was completely supernatural and miraculous. He lifted something from me that had haunted me for years. From that moment on, the heavy breathing was gone and so were the images. They could not hurt me anymore. All I could do was lay there and cry. Thank you Jesus!

My body belonged to the Lord and now it was clean and sanctified. This is the only way I could explain it. I remember going to the Lord in prayer and asking Him, "*Where was the punishment for the men who left their mark on me. How could I forgive them? They took something from me!*" And then He answered, "*Judgement has already fallen and there is no peace within them.*" I needed to forgive and pray for them. Perhaps one day, they too would know the beauty of the Lord. I let this go and left it in the hands of the Lord. Perhaps, maybe, I'll see them in heaven. Only the Lord knows, but I knew I wasn't bound by this anymore.

These were great times for me. I would come to the Lord and just pour out my heart to Him. And then He would come and heal my wounds. I have found that the more we move Christ into our hearts, the more He begins to move things out. Christ begins laying His foundation for us. It is of the utmost importance that He be the One that builds on that foundation.

Matthew 7:24-27
"Therefore whosoever heareth these sayings of mine, and doeth them, I will liken him unto a wise man, which built his house upon a rock: And the rain descended, and the floods came, and the winds blew, and beat upon that house; and it fell not: for it was founded upon a rock. And every one that heareth these sayings of mine, and doeth them not, shall be likened unto a foolish man, which built his house upon the sand: And the rain descended, and the floods came, and the winds blew, and beat upon that house; and it fell: and great was the fall of it."

~fourteen~

Bearing Much Fruit

Ephesians 2:19-22

Now therefore ye are no more strangers and foreigners, but fellow citizens with the saints, and of the household of God; And are built upon the foundation of the apostles and prophets, Jesus Christ himself being the chief corner stone; In whom all the building fitly framed together groweth unto an holy temple in the Lord: In whom ye also are builded together for an habitation of God through the Spirit.

One day, a salesman came to the door selling life insurance. I invited him in and as he delivered his sales pitch, somewhere in the conversation, we began to talk about the Lord. He made a statement I will never forget. "Your daughter isn't going to die of old age," he proclaimed, "but she is going to see the glory of the Lord return." I was greatly moved and affected by what he said and I often think of his words even today. I look forward to the day when I can see the joy on my children's faces when they see the Lord.

Even more amazing to me was being able to witness how the Lord uses His people, everyday people! All that I had expected was a salesman – but this was a ministering salesman! He'll never realize how much life He spoke to me that day, and how much it impacted me.

When we become His light and yield to Him, it will change nations. The Lord desires that we be His Body. And in this Body are many members. We have many brothers and sisters in the Lord and we are all called to be partakers in the Body of Christ. Christ is our head and He is no respecter of persons – He loves us all the same! We're all running toward and enduring for the same prize. Though some may slip, we must learn to help and encourage one another.

I was beginning to become excited about this family of God. I had tons of brothers and sisters. Along this path, I had to learn to love beyond my borders of comfort. I had to learn to love others as Christ loved them. Our family and friends are precious jewels, and this is how Christ sees them. Thank the Lord for others who come along and give us an edifying word, a word of encouragement, or a word of correction. It is a wise man that will take godly counsel, but a proud man will despise it. We are instructed to watch each other's backs. I am so grateful for the sisters I have in Christ. I know that when some say they will pray, they will pray.

We are not here to try and figure this life out on our own. We have instruction on how to live. The Word is the lamp unto our feet! It will light every area of our lives – if we let it. We will build relationships and keep them, and He shows us how to keep them. If we're not keeping relationships, then perhaps it is still a matter of the heart, and it must be dealt with.

There is a time when the Lord will separate you for a season. It will feel like the loneliest time of your life. It will be as if no one is there or understands, but this happens for His glory. This happens to draw you into Him that He may dine and get alone with you. Press in, and stay encouraged, friends will come.

Sometimes, the Lord needs to separate us for awhile from some of our friends who we know are not running with God. Your walk with the Lord needs to be your top priority. And as you grow, you can be that help to those lost friends in their time of need. Begin praying for those whom you love and watch the Lord begin to move. I have lost friends along the way because my heart was focused on the things of the Lord, and I just was not the same anymore. In the Lord's faithfulness, He has brought more friends in. It is hard to find true friends, but trust the Lord, He'll bring others forward. A friend loveth at all times (Proverbs 17:17). Keep your eyes on the Lord and just learn to trust Him.

Philippians 2:3
Let nothing be done through strife or vain-glory; but in lowliness of mind let each esteem other better than themselves.

Putting others before you is indeed a great task. The people of this world will not think twice about stepping over anyone in their way in order to be number one, to be the popular one, to be the one in the spotlight; but in Christ the complete opposite is true. Christ calls us to have humility and to love others. He left us that example. Though He was the Creator of the universe, the Lord of all things, he humbled Himself and washed His disciple's feet. (John 13:14)

2 Corinthians 10:12-13
For we dare not make ourselves of the number, or compare ourselves with some that commend themselves: but they measuring themselves by themselves, and comparing themselves among themselves, are not wise. But we will not boast of things without our measure, but according to the measure of the rule which God hath distributed to us, a measure to reach even unto you.

We need to be reminded from where we once came and that no one is above the other. Let us be encouraged by this. Man can elevate anyone he chooses to, but the Lord is the only one who opens doors for us. And He does this on His time – not ours! Everything is done in His time. No one can speed up this progress. And those who try will be in for a great fall. If you have hindrances in your life that the Lord is dealing with, it is best for you to deal with them! When you get into the Word of God it will truly bless you and encourage you! But above this, it will bring conviction in your life so that you may change into the person God intended you to be.

> **1 Peter 5:6**
> **Humble yourselves therefore under the mighty hand of God, that he may exalt you in due time:**

The Lord will always give you strength to endure any testing. Oftentimes, our trials result in, or come as, hindered relationships. Finding humility in these situations is not always easy. It is pride that keeps us from reconciling the fractured relationship. Pride will always justify itself, stays defensive, and hates to be corrected. When the spirit of humility is upon a person they will always go and make things right, because they do not always have to be right, nor are concerned when they have been wronged. Pride, or the fleshy carnal nature of man, will be quick to cast its judgement upon others. As human beings, we are often so quick to judge and gossip about others. I am guilty of this myself. We often need to be reminded about who is in control and who saved us. Once we become aware of this we must do what the Word of God tells us to do, and that is to repent.

We need to grasp and understand that "walking in Christ" is learned and practiced a little at a time.

We are learning and growing daily, and will continue to grow more into His likeness until we meet Him in glory. Let us help the younger ones, and admonish them with Word and with godly love.

Galatians 6:1
Brethren, if a man be overtaken in a fault, ye which are spiritual, restore such an one in the spirit of meekness; considering thyself, lest thou also be tempted.

If we allow a relationship to go without forgiveness, than we ourselves run the certain risk of becoming bitter. It's important that you make that relationship right before the Lord, because the Lord sees the heart. If there be any brother or sister you have not forgiven, go and make things right with them. Don't allow pride to hinder your walk with the Lord. Let us not become puffed up for love edifies, (1 Corinthians 8:1). Returning to my friend after being offended was sometimes hard to do. Many times, I left them grinding my teeth. I wanted to hurt them and say something too, but with God's help I would hold my tongue.

There have been countless times I have seen the ugliness of the flesh rear up, and I had to turn to the Lord for forgiveness. It's in the prayer closet His love for others will compel you to love them even when others talk about you and do bad things against you. When I've been wronged, I need to make sure no offense is taken and my wounds don't stay open for infection.

You can always tell when someone is in prayer; their love for you is genuine, and friends love all the time. There are times you may be rejected; press in and the Lord will bring you others who will love you as Christ loves. Check your heart and make sure no offenses are hidden.

Matthew 18:7
Woe unto the world because of offences! for it must needs be that offences come; but woe to that man by whom the offence cometh!

When we become offended, the offense will appeal to our pride and rise up. Anger takes its position for defense and this takes root into our heart and can cause division. There is a reason for this Word and edification: it's because when we walk in obedience to this Word, our walk with the Lord will grow deeper.

1 Corinthians 3:1-3
And I, brethren, could not speak unto you as unto spiritual, but as unto carnal, even as unto babes in Christ. I have fed you with milk, and not with meat: for hitherto ye were not able to bear it, neither yet now are ye able. For ye are yet carnal: for whereas there is among you envying, and strife, and divisions, are ye not carnal, and walk as men?

The Lord desires to continue to pour out His wisdom, but, unless we can let go and grow into the likeness of Christ, we will never grow. We will never be fed more than just the milk of the Word and we will not reach the next place Christ desires for us. Love the Lord and obey Him, you will be blessed. If you don't, your walk in Christ will continue to be hindered. When Christ came, He offended many people, because their hearts, full of themselves despised correction and rebuke. We must continually be led by the Holy Spirit. This requires picking up our cross and walking as Christ walked.

Matthew 10:38
"And he that taketh not his cross, and followeth after me, is not worthy of me."

When we learn to die to "self" then it is for our gain. Our family, friends, and neighbours will be saved, and our death to self will touch lives and the world. So often we can praise ourselves and boast in our own works, but are the people around you seeing it? If so, 'Let another man praise you and not your own mouth; a stranger, and not your own lips' (Proverbs 27:2). There are so many who proclaim their own goodness, but who can find a faithful man? (Proverbs 20:6) We must hearken to this and let it be a word for all of us. Let it be Christ that lives and walks in and through us! We must remember that we are not our own any longer. He has bought and purchased us with His own precious blood. Therefore, let us live our lives accordingly – not as our own, but as His.

Galatians 2:20
I am crucified with Christ: nevertheless I live; yet not I, but Christ liveth in me: and the life which I now live in the flesh I live by the faith of the Son of God, who loved me, and gave himself for me.

The purpose of this great life within is for the world. Our lives are meant to reach out to the lost, to encourage, and to be shining lights reflecting the great hope found only in Christ. The closer we draw to the Lord, the more of Christ we will reflect and be. There is only one way to draw close to Him – walk in obedience! By walking in obedience, you will bear much fruit. You will see His beauty in you and so will others.

Galatians 5:22-23
But the fruit of the Spirit is love, joy, peace, longsuffering, gentleness, goodness, faith, meekness, temperance: against such there is no law.

How could men and women miss this? They shop for hours for new clothes and new gadgets, but they are missing the most prized possession given unto us all – Christ Jesus! Sadly, many are losing control of their lives and need help. And yet, the simplicity of the Gospel is within reach to all mankind! The Saviour, and the precious gift of the Holy Spirit, are just a whisper away. The moment we call on Him, He is there.

~fifteen~

Something is Different about Me

Song of Solomon 3:6
Who is this that cometh out of the wilderness like pillars of smoke, perfumed with myrrh and frankincense, with all powders of the merchant?

"I want the old Sonia back!"

My life was changing, and this was becoming clearly evident to Khalil. He was unable to control me, or make me feel unworthy anymore. The relationship had changed. My decisions, and the way I lived, revolved around Jesus now.

Khalil had a place downtown. I would take our daughter there so they could visit, but I was always uneasy and always on edge. One day, when Hasslina and I were at Khalil's place visiting, Khalil and I ended up arguing. I decided to leave. As I was getting ready to go to the door, Khalil became very angry. He started yelling and jumping up and down and began hitting his head with his hands, over and over again. Frightened by this display, I scooped up Hasslina and got out of there as quickly as I could. It wasn't until sometime later Khalil told me what had happened. He told me he had heard voices. They had told him to throw me off the balcony. It was because of this night that I knew I had an enemy who wanted to destroy me. Thankfully, I had the Lord's hand over my life.

My walk with the Lord was disturbing Khalil greatly. The closer I walked with Jesus, the less we had to say to one another. All I wanted to do was talk about the Lord and all that He was doing in my life. I no longer had any interest in the things Khalil and I used to talk about and enjoy doing. The things of the world, all the things that I once used to enjoy before, had become extremely dim in the light of Jesus Christ.

2 Corinthians 6:14
Be ye not unequally yoked together with unbelievers: for what fellowship hath righteousness with unrighteousness? And what communion hath light with darkness?

How, Lord, am I ever going to be free from Khalil?

This was still an area of my life I needed help with. I had given birth to his daughter, and I knew that he was going to be a part of our lives for a very long time. He was still trying to control and tell me how to do things. His behaviour infuriated me. The situation remained the same. What was I going to do? I knew that having him in our lives would surely destroy us. I didn't know what to do. *He had threatened the kids and me. Where shall we go? What were we going to do?*

I talked to my mom about it and she asked me, "Sonia, do you pray for him?" Had I? For some reason I hadn't. I fully believed that he was never going to change. He was a Muslim! I knew that Muslims would not and did not accept and believe the gospel of Jesus Christ. I had bought him an Arabic Bible but, he didn't seem very interested in it. It lay on top of his fridge collecting dust. I had to trust that what the Lord was doing in my life, He was able to do in Khalil's life as well.

Over time, I knew that the Lord was going to do something amazing. As it was for now, whenever I mentioned Christ to him, his argument was always the same: it was impossible to have a personal relationship with God, especially a close relationship! God was too holy to come and interact with us. He just could not fathom this personal relationship I had with Christ. Although I understood his argument, I had to give him to the Lord and continue to administer the Word of the Lord in love. All I could do was trust the Lord to open the truth to him.

God is Holy and it is only by His Son, Jesus Christ, who stands as our advocate before the Father and intercedes on our behalf, (1 John 2:1) that we can stand before God. Because of Jesus, we are able to have a personal relationship with God the Father.

It is the Holy Spirit who knocks and waits for us to open our hearts to Christ Jesus. Once we open up to Him, He comes in and dines with us (Rev 3:20). Christ cares for every part of our life. He gives us the power to come into the presence of God and boldly share our heart and talk with God. In His faithfulness, He will come and restore us and make us whole. God didn't give us this eternal and abundant life so we could walk alone! We could never do it alone in our own strength.

The Israelite children lived under the law. Before faith came, we were kept under guard by the law, kept for the faith which would afterwards be revealed. Therefore, the law was our tutor to bring us to Christ, that we might be justified by faith. After faith has come, we are no longer under a tutor (Galatians 3:23-25).

Now, walking by faith – having our sin exposed by the law – enabled by the Holy Spirit, we are more than able to walk in obedience, righteousness, and holiness, and walk just as Christ walked, (1 John 2:6).

More than anything else, Khalil was noticing the power of God in my life and the change it had brought forth. I had changed right before his eyes! It was the testimony of my life that ministered to him.

In December 2003, he received word that his father had passed away. Khalil was lost and upset. He never had had the chance to really talk with his father. He had held on to too many painful memories, and now he had no chance of ever saying goodbye. Anger had filled his heart because his father had never been the father Khalil had hoped for. Yet in the midst of this anger Khalil mourned. His dad was gone – forever.

Later that week I received a call from Khalil. The words he spoke through the phone were words I never thought I would hear from him. He invited me over and told me he wanted to accept Jesus into his heart. My heart and soul were dancing at the news of this and so we arranged to meet the next day. I asked my sister Abby to come along with me and take part in witnessing this miracle.

This was such an amazing testimony for Jesus. When we went into his apartment and gathered around to go into prayer, the presence of the Lord fell into that little room. Tears streamed down his face. It was amazing to watch the Lord set him free. This man, who had been so cruel and mean at times, was becoming a new man right before my eyes.

When we had spoken on the phone the previous day, Khalil told me of a dream he'd had the night before. It was a nightmare, and I knew it had really put fear into him. He described his dream to me. He saw a table. He stood on one side; on the other side of the table stood a figure which seemed god-like. On the table sat two books. One was the Q'uran and the other was the Bible. In his dream, this god-like figure asked him which one he believed in. Khalil answered, "Jesus." This god-like person then became enraged at his answer and threw the table over and declared to Khalil "for this you are going to hell!" Disturbed and frightened by this he woke up. When he tried to go back to sleep, he felt his head being pushed down into his pillow. I knew that we needed to pray over this. In agreement, we declared and prayed the Word over Khalil. In the name of Jesus we commanded the dreams to leave.

Finally free after 36 yrs! He can now sleep with the light out. The nightmares are gone and he enjoys his sleep now. It was amazing to watch! I often think of this miracle when hard times come. I had truly witnessed a miracle. I never thought that would happen. Now I know that what is impossible with man, is possible with God. Khalil rejoices with me now, he knows for certain his daughter will one day see God and His fullness. Since that day, he has never cursed or threatened my children or me again. To God be the glory! This was a miracle!

With all the amazing things the Lord was doing in my life, how could I remain quiet?

I received a phone call from Khalil a few days after he accepted the Lord. "Sonia," he exclaimed, "What did you do to me? I can feel Jesus all over me and He's with me wherever I go. I can't say or do no wrong. It's like He's here watching me!" I could only smile. I loved watching his excitement. He was so thankful for what the Lord had done. Prayers for his family in Iraq could begin now.

The U.S.-led war with Iraq had been watched by the world. It was an emotional time for Khalil. He had to watch from afar and his worries were on his family back home. He knew the extent of their suffering. He was in Iraq during the Gulf War. He and his fellow soldiers escaped when they could. Khalil had escaped into Turkey. He came to Canada in 1993 and lived here since. I listened as he would share stories about the tyrannical leader Saddam Hussein, Iraq's former dictator. He recounted how his people suffered horribly at the hands of this madman. His stories were so disturbing that I asked him not to tell me anymore. So when the war broke out in Iraq and Saddam's regime crumbled, Khalil had the chance to witness his people celebrate out on the street. This dictator had everything a man could want. He lived in a palace and lived like a king. Sadly, the people of Iraq lacked basic medical care and were subjected to cruelty at his evil hands. Unfortunately, there are still many countries with suffering citizens under a cruel dictatorship.

On December 31, 2005, Khalil, and the world, watched as this former dictator was executed. Khalil felt temporary satisfaction and overjoyed until reality hit his heart and he felt deep sorrow. The man, who had lived like a king, had been hunted like an animal and found in a hole in the ground. Ironically, after a swift trial he was executed with his own familiar method, hanging. It didn't have to end like this.

Christ is the only one who can save our souls. Salvation does not come by wealth or through fame. It is only through Jesus that we are saved. Nothing else on earth or in heaven can save you! Salvation comes only through Jesus.

Acts 4:12
Neither is there salvation in any other: for there is none other name under heaven given among men, whereby we must be saved.

One thing I know of this great and mighty King that sits on high, is that His love abounds for all. We who are saved have a job to do. We are to be a light in a darkened world. We are called to go into all the world and share this good news.

In all things there is a season; a time of maturing and growing. I didn't understand everything that was happening, but I knew in my heart that the Lord was doing something.

~sixteen~

Times of Testing

Jeremiah 17:10
I the LORD search the heart, I try the reins, even to give every man according to his ways, and according to the fruit of his doings.

Little was I aware that ahead of me were trials and times of great testing. *Would my love for God cause me to forge ahead or would these trials and tests harden my heart?* At times, I didn't know why things were happening the way they were. It seemed that my Lord had left me. *Was I going to continue to trust Him?*

With the murders and other things that were happening in my area, I decided on getting a dog for protection. I found Jade. She was a beautiful German Shepherd. The kids loved her, and being a single parent, I felt better with her in the house. Although I had chosen her for protection and security, I did not know that she was going to be a reason for the next battle in my life.

A year after I moved into a housing complex there was a particular neighbour, a woman, who just seemed to make problems for everyone. My heart went out to those people she bullied on. I had no issues with her – until the following year. It was now my turn to be bullied on.

This lady had a little Jack Russell terrier that would sprint out the front door the moment it opened. And because the little dog was so quick, she was hard to catch. One evening, Hassan asked me if he could go out to the car to fetch something he had forgotten. Moments later, he came running in, screaming. He started yelling at Jade to sit down, but Jade was upset at this lady's little Jack Russell. Like all dogs, Jade was territorial, and she was upset with this little dog that had set foot on her territory. Jade barked and barked some more until this little dog was out of sight. I pulled Jade back in and shut the door. 'Incident over.' Or so I thought.

Later that evening, I decided to take Jade out for her run. As we crossed the parking lot to my car, I could hear someone cursing at me from across the parking lot. It was her. I couldn't believe the nerve of this woman! She was blaming my dog for chasing her Jack Russell on the road that, unfortunately, had gotten struck and killed by a passing car. The whole incident was an ugly one. As much as I tried to tell her, she would not believe me that my dog had been leashed the whole time. Her daughters had told her that Jade had been without a leash and had chased her dog into the street. Their false accusations had made me look like a liar and, in her eyes, a dog murderer.

The argument was intense and I thought we were going to get physical right there in the parking lot. The kids were crying and Jade was frantically barking. I thought she was going to fly through the car window. Jade was upset that someone was yelling at me. I could feel the anger rising up within me and I was quite sure now that I was going to get physical. It was at that moment I felt the Lord's presence. I turned and looked and saw the kids crying. I knew I had to leave right then and there.

My neighbours had heard the intense arguing and they started coming out to see what the commotion was about. It wasn't long before they started arguing with this lady as well. This woman had problems with so many neighbours! She was being hit up from all directions. With the neighbours arriving on the scene I was finally able to leave, but not before I said some things to her.

Once away from that ugly scene we drove to a place I had found. I had discovered a nice secluded spot for Jade and the kids to run and play without any fear of vehicles. Jade could run and enjoy her freedom. We loved it there! But when I arrived that evening, my nerves were shot. I couldn't believe what had just happened. Why was this happening?

Why God, would you allow this? I'm going to hurt this lady.

I was so upset. Revenge and retaliation filled my mind. I was so angry. I thought of calling a few friends to come over. My mind was racing. How was I going to handle this woman? The ugly thoughts that surfaced kept me in prayer. I knew what the 'Old Sonia' would have done. But I was a daughter of God now. I had to stay in prayer. When I finished praying, my anger was lifted. I knew my battle was spiritual. I wasn't fighting flesh and blood.

Ephesians 6:12
For we wrestle not against flesh and blood, but against principalities, against powers, against the rulers of the darkness of this world, against spiritual wickedness in high places.

There was a spirit that wanted me to strike back and fight physically. The enemy knew my weaknesses and was setting me up for a fall. Was I going to have to fight again? Yes! But I was going to learn how to fight on my knees through prayer.

When it was time to head home, I hoped that she had calmed down. As we arrived back, she was still outside. Her house unit was almost directly behind mine and her parking spot was one over from mine. The moment we pulled up, she came over to my car. I knew her verbal attacks were coming and as soon as I opened my door, they started. I just continued to ignore her and went inside the house with my children and Jade.

From that moment on, it seemed she came at me every time we went somewhere. She would watch my going in and coming out, leisurely, from her window. I was so angry that, at times, my body would tremble and then I would cry. I felt helpless and didn't understand why the Lord was allowing this to happen to me? I called the police and told them the things that were happening, but that did no good. When the police officer went to go talk with her, he came back to me with another story. That was when I knew that this situation was worse than I thought. This lady was something else! This whole situation left me in disbelief.

One night, Hassan called to me from the top of the stairs. He was in tears. He told me that when he was looking outside his window she gave him 'the finger.' I wanted her hurt. How ignorant! Then I went to the office of the MP of our area, but this didn't help none either. The property management couldn't get rid of her, their hands were tied to. In fact, it amazed me how long she was able to keep her place. I'm not sure what she said or did to keep her unit as long as she did, but she was able to. Everything seemed so surreal.

Many times, I fell to my knees and cried out "Help us Lord!" This was hurting me so bad. Then to make matters worse, my car started to give me problems. Everything seemed to come against me from all directions and she enjoyed every minute of it. She had front row seats to watch my car give me problem after problem. At one time, my car was even squealing whenever I shut if off! I still have no idea, what it was that caused it, but it was embarrassing to say the least. When my alternator went, she sat there laughing at me. When my car would choke, she sat there laughing at me. I knew the Lord was somewhere, but I often asked where He was. Why was this happening to me? Why was He allowing it to happen to me? I knew I had two choices, and I knew that if I reacted and became physical, I would be incarcerated and who would look after my kids?

One beautiful summer day, she was there to greet me again as I came home. When I arrived this time, I put the kids inside the house and went back to my car. I was shaking and seething, but she didn't say a word to me. I remember her standing only a few feet away from me, and it took everything inside me to keep walking back to the house. I walked into my house through my back entrance which led into my kitchen. I put on some worship music in the CD player I had atop my fridge. I had to go into prayer, or I was going to lose it. I couldn't take it anymore.

Lord! She was still there and I could still see her, she was only a few feet away. I just started praying and weeping because of weariness. "*Oh God, you know my enemy is outside my door. Help me Lord!* When I said those words, His presence filled my kitchen. As I prayed, although she stood just outside my door, she seemed like a thousand miles away. The next thing that happened was hard to believe – I was hearing myself praying for her, and for her kids. I was praying for blessings to be poured abundantly upon them and that they would find Jesus. Consuming love for her continued to pour into me and I felt nothing but compassion for her and her family. My heart ached for them. I knew then what God was doing. He was showing me His heart. If I wanted to know and walk in Him, I needed to know His heart, and His heart was still on the lost.

Luke 19:10
"For the Son of Man is come to seek and to save that which was lost."

I knew the Lord was also humbling me and teaching me continually to put off the former man. This street mentality that had been rooted down in me needed to be uprooted. I couldn't handle things my way and if I continued in my ways, my dream would become real. I would go to prison or someone would kill me. I was being tested and tried while the Lord was continuing to work in me.

I felt this warring in my soul and I'm glad I surrendered to the Lord. Because of my obedience, the Lord filled my heart with such love for this woman and her family.

To know the heart of God means loving even our enemies. Christ died and rose again for her too and I needed to be His light and His testimony. I wasn't going to react the way I used to anymore. The Lord was giving me a complete heart change. Choosing who we love is never an option. We are called to bless those who hate and persecute us.

Matthew 5:44
"But I say unto you, Love your enemies, bless them that curse you, do good to them that hate you, and pray for them which despitefully use you, and persecute you;"

I'm not sure where this woman is today, but I soon realized that the Lord had placed her in my life to be a blessing to me. I will encounter many more like her and will be tried and tested, but I must remember the gospel of Jesus Christ. We are to love our neighbour and to love one another. If I didn't have the Lord to turn to, I would have hardened my heart and maybe I would be locked in a jail cell today. Out of His mercy, He showed me what it means to walk in the Spirit. When I walked in Him, I was able to pray and love this lady. Who else was praying for her? Who was going to start interceding for her? Christ died for all of us, and no matter how difficult some people may be, we must love them.

When we become transformed, people will want to know what has happened in us. Christ in His goodness will stir your heart for others that we may minister hope unto others.

John 7:38
"He that believeth on me, as the scripture hath said, out of his belly shall flow rivers of living water."

It seemed wherever I went and wherever I looked there were others who needed prayer or just someone to listen to them. I was able to give hope to others by ministering the Word now. It is crucial for lovers of Christ to consume and know the Word of God. In due time, the Lord will begin to open scriptures up to us. With each new scripture I was learning, I had to walk through it. I wasn't just going to quote scripture – I was going to live it!

> **Colossians 2:5-8**
> **For though I be absent in the flesh, yet am I with you in the spirit, joying and beholding your order, and the stedfastness of your faith in Christ. As ye have therefore received Christ Jesus the Lord, so walk ye in him: Rooted and built up in him, and stablished in the faith, as ye have been taught, abounding therein with thanksgiving. Beware lest any man spoil you through philosophy and vain deceit, after the tradition of men, after the rudiments of the world, and not after Christ.**

I was going to know the Word. I knew that the Lord intended that my learning would not be taught by men, but by His Spirit (Galatians 1:12). Perhaps I had heard the Word preached before and, of course, when the Word is preached it is good, but it's the revelation of God's Word that changes us. Men can teach and preach the Word, but if it's not anointed by the Spirit, we're missing the mark. We must continue to walk in Christ, drawing closer to Him through prayer and praise. When we draw near to Him, He will draw near to us.

1 Peter 4:12
Beloved, think it not strange concerning the fiery trial which is to try you, as though some strange thing happened unto you:

May we walk through the Word and, by the Word, run the course the Lord has set before us. Don't be discouraged when the trials come. All that we endure is for the glory of God, and through it we will be strengthened.

Galatians 4:19
My little children, of whom I travail in birth again until Christ be formed in you,

His purpose in all our obstacles is that He may be our all in all. The transformation in my life was beginning to show and others were taking notice. Instead of a dead dandelion, I was blooming into something beautiful. It wasn't my beauty of course, but the Lord's.

There is nothing in the world that can compare to the life of Christ when He lives within our heart. Although the world may be blinded we must continue to press in and push through. Regardless of what new fads and new things come, or, how well people are covered up, the world is still hurting. My eyes have opened more now to the hurting world around me. It seems everywhere I turn, someone needs to hear a word of hope or encouragement. And everywhere, someone needs prayer.

~seventeen~

Time to Let the Light Shine

John 12:32
"And I, if I be lifted up from the earth, will draw all men unto me."

When we become more Christ-like, it will draw others unto Him. They may not be able to explain it, but they will know something is different about you. I started to run into familiar people whom I had run the streets with. My friend Dee was one of the first.

I was driving down the strip where I once used to buy drugs. This was the same strip that I would stagger home from. When I saw from where I had come from, I was in complete disbelief. *"I praise you Lord!"* Nothing could have changed me and saved me, except the blood of Christ.

When I came to the end of the street I saw my old friend Dee. It looked as if she was getting ready to cross the road. I rolled my window down, called out to her, and offered her a ride home. We were so happy to see each other. I told her I was serving the Lord and all the great things that were happening to me. She was somewhat taken aback. She said that she used to go to church, but that this was her life now. I just wanted to hug her and take her home with me, but I knew she was in the Lord's hands and I had done what I was supposed to. I knew this was a time that the Lord had ordained. In an hour when she needs someone, I know that she will remember our meeting. All it takes is a testimony for the Lord and the person to whom you have ministered will never forget. I love this girl and she will continue to be in my prayers. Perhaps the next time Dee and I will see each other will be in heaven. Meeting her this day and driving through the block reminded me of all that the Lord had taken me out of. I was so thankful to be alive to talk about it.

This desire to shine the Lord to the world caused my mom and I to work together toward a business plan. We started going to the library downtown to work on this business plan for "G.O.D. Designs." Our purpose was to open a storefront for our plaques and frames. Let's just say we had fun trying to do it. We had our business luncheons weekly. These meetings proved to be productive in the sense that my mom and I were drawn closer together. We had many good laughs because our daily luncheon meetings were mainly increasing our waistlines. As for being business minded and entrepreneurial, we still had much to learn. It was a time in our lives that I would never change.

One day, while waiting for mom to arrive for one of our business meetings, I waited patiently while reading through some material. It was then that I saw a friend I used to party and hang out with. I could see he was in bad shape. I went over and started talking with him. He told me he used the library as his shelter to stay warm because he didn't have his own place. He would wait around for his drinking buddies to show up and they would go and hustle for their next drink. My heart went out for my friend and this opened the door to minister life to him.

He didn't look like he had bathed lately and I could see his embarrassment. He was one person I knew that always took pride in his appearance and his beautiful white teeth. I couldn't believe this was him...I just wanted to hug him. I knew that he was also of Muslim faith, but after I had seen the power of God transform Khalil, I had no doubt that Christ could do the same for my friend. When the Lord moves on a heart, *who can deny Him*?

It was on another trip to the library that I saw my friend again. This time, I invited him to go for coffee. We went and had coffee and something to eat. Afterward we decided to go for a walk. I could feel the Spirit beginning to stir – I knew the Lord was going to move. When we got to the park downtown, we stopped and sat on a park bench. I talked to him about how the Lord could change his life. When I asked him if he wanted to accept Christ into his life, he said "Yes."

Luke 15:10
"Likewise, I say unto you, there is joy in the presence of the angels of God over one sinner that repenteth."

I was so happy for him and then I told him about David Wilkerson. I shared his testimony and how he had founded Teen Challenge. I knew it blessed my friend to hear this. The Lord is looking for vessels to go and do His will – His desire is to use us. Later, I went and picked up a little paperback copy of David Wilkerson's book, *The Cross and the Switchblade*. I gave it to my friend and I knew he was encouraged by this. He kept it in his back pocket and he really seemed to treasure this little book. He was excited and I knew he was in God's hands.

A couple of weeks went by, and I still hadn't gone to the library. The day I decided to go in, I saw my friend walking toward me and he was smiling and happy. I knew it was this new life in Christ that had him grinning from ear to ear. He said to me, "When you share with me, it keeps me going." I could see it in his face; the Word was bringing him life. This man was beginning to become spiritually hungry and I was blessed. I asked him if he had finished reading *The Cross and The Switchblade*. He said, "Yes." Oh how I wanted to take him aside and shield him from all harm, but he was in the Father's hands.

Whenever we share the Good News, His Word does not return to Him void. His Word is sharper than a double edged sword and cuts down to the very heart. We don't walk alone. You must have faith when you share the gospel of Jesus. I've learned that when you call on His name He will be there. Minister the gospel in love and share what God has been doing in your own life. Christ will always bring a testimony to the changed life that they see in you.

> **1 Peter 3:15**
> **But sanctify the Lord God in your hearts: and be ready always to give an answer to every man that asketh you a reason of the hope that is in you with meekness and fear:**

There are others, of course, who will run from you.

> **2 Corinthians 2:15-16**
> **For we are unto God a sweet savour of Christ, in them that are saved, and in them that perish: To the one we are the savour of death unto death; and to the other the savour of life unto life.**

And there are some who will run from the light.

> **John 3:19-21**
> **"And this is the condemnation, that light is come into the world, and men loved darkness rather than light, because their deeds were evil. For every one that doeth evil hateth the light, neither cometh to the light, lest his deeds should be reproved. But he that doeth truth cometh to the light, that his deeds may**

be made manifest, that they are wrought in God."

Not everyone we meet will accept God or hear what we have to say. Many will hate us, for within us is light, and this light will shine upon their darkened lives. A heart immersed in sin, will not come to the light, therefore it will despise you. The Word even goes further and declares that we will be hated by all men for His sake; but he that shall endure unto the end, the same shall be saved (Mark 13:13).

Even lukewarm carnal Christians will persecute them who love Christ. A Christian on fire for God will cast light onto the hidden sin in the carnal Christian's life. The further we go in Christ, and the closer we get to Him, the more Christ-like we'll become. The more I continued to draw into the Lord, the more friends I had to let go. Our lives became so different that we had nothing more in common. All I wanted to do was talk about Christ and I had no desire to talk about anything else. I lost all desire of the former things I once enjoyed, and now my only passion was my Lord and Saviour, Jesus Christ.

I am not writing this book to become popular because the Lord knows that I have already lost some friends along the way. I write because there is a love and a fire within my heart to warn you that there is judgment coming. There is also a reward to them that seek and love Him. God's love for us is beyond our limited human comprehension. His love gives life so we must take heed to His Word. I have run into friends who have made some ignorant remarks toward me.

In their minds they saw me as "going religious." One close friend came and whispered in my ear, "I hear you're going religious." He really meant no harm and it made me smile. I was completely unashamed. I wasn't being religious. I was in love. I had a relationship that he didn't know nor understood. In my heart, I knew I had to love him, not cast judgment, and continue to shine the Lord's love.

One evening, as I lay on my bed, I read the newspaper and was heartbroken to read of another tragedy. The story was of a young mother who had been murdered by her ex-boyfriend. She had lived just down the street from us. My heart broke for her. I knew the fear she must have lived with. She had been only 17 years old. The paper reported that she had split with her boyfriend. In his rage, he came to her apartment and opened fire upon her, killing her and leaving behind their baby. There are sad, tragic, and heartbreaking stories like this every day, in every city, and in every country. In the past few years, it feels like evil has been seeping faster into our city streets. Or perhaps, it was that I had been just too desensitized to have noticed this evil before. Our world is in dire need of the Saviour! Stories like this continue to make me weep and cry before the Lord. "*What can I do? Lord, have mercy on us.*"

Stories like this have helped me to put into perspective how evil continues to reign in the hearts and minds of men. Every day many are losing their lives. Christ has bought and purchased us, and we do not have to live as slaves to sin any longer. But many are selling themselves for nothing (Isaiah 52:3). They are selling themselves for quick satisfactions, and are more interested in the here and now. Many don't know His truth and His promise of eternal salvation. My heart's cry was for the Lord to use me. *How can you use me Lord?* As I flipped through the Word that evening, a scripture in Ezekiel stopped me in my tracks.

Ezekiel 33:6
"But if the watchman see the sword come, and blow not the trumpet, and the people be not warned; if the sword come, and take any person from among them, he is taken away in his iniquity; but his blood will I require at the watchman's hand."

What I had in my life wasn't for me to keep — I was commissioned to minister the Word and preach the gospel! Each of us is expected to do so. We can share it anywhere — at work, school, at the gym — anywhere! You can share the gospel with any person the Lord puts before you. It is always for God's purpose and for His glory. What I had, I couldn't contain, and it was bubbling out wherever I went. I write now only to give the Lord honour and to give hope to others. I don't fully know where these words will go, but it will go to wherever the Lord sends it. This book is in your hands today because the Lord desires to minister to your heart. I know and pray that there will be no blood on my hands on Judgment Day. I will continually declare the Word and how He saved me. His eyes are on you and me, and on many others who are hurting right now.

There is a battle. I am beginning to understand that the more we press in with the Word, the more the opposition increases against us. I never understood why so many sisters and brothers in Christ suffered for the gospel and what moved them. Now I know. It is love for others. Though the gates of hell may shake, they shall not prevail against the Church (Matthew 16:18). And though you may have many challenges and may endure things you don't sometimes understand, you and I need to keep going and remember that the Lord is in control. A spiritual war is being fought for our souls; let us not be ignorant to the adversary's devices (2 Corinthians 2:11). The things we endure are to strengthen us and save our very souls. Some say not to worry about what our enemy is doing, but the Word says otherwise. We cannot be ignorant of His devices. We must be aware of how the enemy comes in subtly. We need to know his schemes and ways are meant to thwart us off God's path and to bring us into deception.

Jeremiah 12:5
If thou hast run with the footmen, and they have wearied thee, then how canst thou contend with horses? And if in the land of peace, wherein thou trustedst, they wearied thee, then how wilt thou do in the swelling of Jordan?

One night I dreamt I was looking outside my bedroom window toward the sky, and I could see numerous dark clouds coming toward me. They were raging back and forth and the sight of it was very frightening, but I remember that I wasn't afraid. Later that week, I went to my pastor and asked him what he thought it meant. He said it was for me. "Pray," he said, "pray."

~eighteen~

The Waves Begin

Psalm 23:1-5

The LORD is my shepherd; I shall not want. He maketh me to lie down in green pastures: he leadeth me beside the still waters. He restoreth my soul: he leadeth me in the paths of righteousness for his name's sake. Yea, though I walk through the valley of the shadow of death, I will fear no evil: for thou art with me; thy rod and thy staff they comfort me. Thou preparest a table before me in the presence of mine enemies: thou anointest my head with oil; my cup runneth over.

I was in my new place for about six months when I received a phone call from family in Saskatchewan concerning my grandmother. *Kokum* was very sick and in the hospital. She needed help. There was no one else in the family that was able to go to her at the time, and I knew in my heart that I had to go back.

It had been a couple of years since I had last seen her. I knew it was time to see her again. I missed her terribly. I wondered how long I would be there. I wasn't sure, but I knew things in my life were going to change.

Whenever I thought of the reserve, I wasn't too anxious to go back. I had some bad childhood memories from out there; not of Kokum, but of other things that happened to us. I had been planning to go to Mount Zion International School of Ministry in Pennsylvania which had been founded by David Wilkerson. And so I wondered, how long would I be on the reserve?

We made some arrangements and my uncle came from Saskatchewan to pick us up. Everything happened so quickly! I didn't have time to put my things into storage, so my mom stepped in and helped me out.

I had to find a place for Jade. I wasn't going to have a place of my own so it wasn't a good idea to bring her. I didn't think *Kokum* would have liked having Jade there. It was easier to just find Jade a home. This was hard to do because I loved her so much. She was such a beautiful dog; I knew I was going to miss her. The way she tilted her head to side to side, and the way she always stayed by my side, had wooed my heart to fall in love with her. It was hard to let her go.

I wasn't married, and with letting Jade go, I had nothing to hold me back in Ontario. Lately, there hadn't been anything but problems between myself and my son's dad and his new wife. The strife and fighting between us was causing Hassan grief, so it was a good idea to leave for a while. My kids would have to wait for the holidays for visits. I was so thankful they didn't have any tears. They were excited.

The trip to Saskatchewan went well. It felt good to be on Key reserve again. I couldn't wait to see *Kokum*! When I finally did see her, I was saddened to see how much weight she had lost. I hugged her and kissed her. I was so glad to have this time with her. We would sit up late together, share stories, laugh, and have a good cup of tea.

To me, she was the greatest grandmother in the world, and I loved her dearly. She had been taking care of one of her grandsons since he was about two years old. She had taken him in and loved him like her own. I could see that she was doing an amazing job. He was 15 years old and he was her pride and joy. He was a tall, slender, dark, and handsome boy. He was involved in sports and was a promising athlete.

Once I settled in, I would run him to his games and do her errands in town. After a short time, she got her strength back and she was back to her old self. It was time to look at other housing arrangements. My children and I were all sharing one room so things were becoming difficult.

My aunt and uncle who lived close by were ministers. Their church was set up beautifully right on their property. The place was stunning. They ran a Christian school and so I was able to send my kids there. It was all so nice. I had always wanted my children in a Christian school, so this was an answered prayer. I was able to help out at the school whenever possible. It felt so good to be around family and to be able to get close to them. My aunt had another house that they used as a game room on their property and I asked if I could use it. She knew of our situation and she warmly opened her doors for us. We now had our own house.

Although we needed our space I was feeling a little apprehensive about moving in because I knew there was some history between *Kokum* and my aunt. When you are a child, you hear things that you don't quite understand. You know what you hear is bad, but it's quietly pushed away and hopefully forgotten. It wasn't until years later that I would understand and witness the repercussions of a bad testimony. Now here I was back on the reserve again, and it felt like I was slapped back in the middle of this bad situation. I was reminded of it all over again.

Years earlier, *Kokum* had witnessed the emergence of an adulterous affair. She saw it rise up and flourish into a ministry that was seemingly prospering. It was something that she could not understand. And because of it, I knew her heart had become hardened. It was all a twisted triangle that involved my aunt on my father's side, my *Kokum's* son, and her nephew. I didn't know what to say to her. I felt torn between my aunt and *Kokum* because they both were family and I loved them both with all my heart.

What could I say? How was I going to try to explain something I never understood?

The only thing I could do was to give it to the Lord. I could only pray that, in due time, the Lord would soften *Kokum's* heart so she could come to a place of forgiveness. It still left me wondering and asking if this bad testimony was going to cost my grandmother's salvation. How many others had this affected? My heart was broken...for my aunt and the others who were hurt at the end of all this. *How could they be wrong? Were they wrong?*

When the day came to move into my cute little house, I saw a picture of the "Ten Commandments" leaning against the wall. When I saw this, it stirred my heart. I knew the Lord was reminding me of His vision that He had given. I knew I was where I needed to be.

John 10:29
"My Father, which gave them me, is greater than all; and no man is able to pluck them out of my Father's hand."

After a short time, I knew something just wasn't right. The message I was hearing from their ministry did not sit well with me for some reason. I soon realized that my family was preaching another message. More and more I began to understand that what they were preaching was the "prosperity message." I knew it was a message preached prevalently around the world, but I wasn't comfortable with it. Although the message sounded good and outwardly looked good, I knew it wasn't good. I had nothing against prosperity because I knew the Lord desires to bless His children and He does.

This doctrine, however, denies the cross. It does not teach us that as servants of God we are to pick up our crosses. It is a teaching that caters to the flesh and leaves the inward man untouched. The big problem with this is that whenever one denies the cross, the flesh, with its lusts, has room to grow. It is a doctrine that lifts up the flesh and puffs up the heart. I was in an uncomfortable spot and didn't understand why I was here. All I knew was that I didn't want to be in the middle of it.

"Lord, why am I here? I didn't want to be here, I wanted to go to Bible College."

Although we both believed in the name of Jesus, my family was carrying and preaching another kind of gospel. The messages they preached were of "gain." Their messages proclaimed that "gain" was godliness (1Timothy 6:5). As much as I wanted to walk along with them, I knew I couldn't. There was a fine line being drawn. I knew I could not and would not compromise what I knew to be the truth of God's Word. I knew this was an area that grieved God's heart.

I really battled because I knew my family loved the Lord and this was a little too much for me. I was still a babe in Christ and there was still so much for me to learn. Whatever path the Lord wanted me to walk I was going to walk it in obedience. All I knew was that the Lord wanted me just to love my family.

In my own walk with the Lord, I was learning to give things up. I was walking deeper with the Lord. It was within this time, that I saw the covetousness in my own heart. I knew I had been bound. My possessions had me, rather than me having them. My wealth was found within my heart and what my family was ministering seemed contrary to what I was learning in Christ. I knew the treasure I held within my heart was worth much more than all the wealth of the world. This meant having contentment whether I was rich or poor. Obtaining Christ was what made me rich. The richness of Christ cannot be measured by wealth.

Being on the reserve was quiet and beautiful. I wasn't in the city anymore where everything was drowned out by the noise of the city. I didn't have my cell phone, my vehicle, or my name brand coffee; I realized how catered and spoiled I was. I was now able to focus and give more of myself to the Lord rather than living for myself. I was entering into another season. I was shaking off my earthly goods to walk deeper. I was learning to pick up the cross that my family seemed to deny.

Away from home and in new territory, I enjoyed my long walks and took in all the beauty of God's creation. Living on a First Nation reserve wasn't that bad and I was beginning to love it. It gave me the chance to sing and pray my heart out because there wasn't anyone around.

I needed to learn how to press in and grow. I was going to do it one day at a time. The Lord was going to walk with me all the way. Everything was going to be okay – despite what lay ahead.

It was then that I met Rick.

Rick was the right hand man for my family's ministry. He loved the Lord and loved to worship in song. It seemed that at every banquet and dinner we ended up sitting together. Somehow we were drawn together. I knew that Rick had been in a relationship not long before, so I had my guard up. I wasn't sure of being involved with anyone at this point in my life, but I knew my aunt and uncle wanted us together. Rick and I decided that we needed to pray and seek the Lord.

My convictions about the Lord and my family's message caused me to question whether I should become involved with Rick. I battled because if he was under their covering then he obviously shared their teaching. However, different circumstances gave us time to get to know one another and really talk heart to heart. While I listened to his heart, I knew he felt the same way I did and was grieved for the things he was witnessing in the church. His burden, he said, was for the lost. He told me he had the heart of a watchman and wanted to preach truth. With this question eased in my mind, we started seeking confirmation from the Lord. And then things just started to happen.

Fathers Day, June 2005

My uncle decided to hold a baptism by the river and among those being baptized were Hassan and Rick. The day couldn't have been more beautiful. After the baptism took place we headed back to the house to shower and change. Once the kids were back outside, someone went and locked the door. When I turned to see what was going on, Rick's son and his fiancé were grinning from ear to ear. I knew something was definitely up. Rick came out from the bathroom. He came towards me and asked me to come and sit down.

I sat on the couch. As he kneeled before me, he took my hand into his, and then ever so gently he placed a beautiful ring onto my finger. I felt my face flush – this was the way I had always envisioned my engagement. This was beautiful. "Will you marry me?" he asked. My mind flooded with his promises. I saw how he would fill the fatherly role for my children. I saw that he would be a godly husband. I knew that this was answered prayer. Knowing and realizing all of this, I answered "*Yes*." It was a wonderful day for us.

We announced our engagement in the church and everyone was happy. We had planned to get married in the summer – if we had the finances – and that was only a couple of months away. Rick was working as a contractor on the reserve so we just had to prepare and wait. Things looked promising, Rick was a man after the Lord's heart and I was falling in love.

A few months later when the kids were finished school we headed out east to London. We were going back home to visit and gather the remainder of our things while Rick, alongside my family, was ministering on Canada's east coast.

I looked forward to ministering alongside him and often thought about our future. I was confident that he was going to be a good husband and I was finally looking forward to becoming a wife. I was going to make him happy.

We were out east for almost three weeks when we received another phone call from back west; *Kokum* was back in the hospital. This time, her health was worse. I remember going out for a long walk to talk with God. I was screaming inside and trying to push aside all these thoughts of death. I wanted to be assured that she was going to be ok.

My mom, who was still living in Ontario, had decided to come back with us and so we both put our belongings into storage. I stayed with a friend the night before we had planned to leave and waited there for my mom to come for us. My mom drove up in the car we were going to drive halfway across the country in – a 1992 Ford Festiva! Maybe this is an understatement, but it was a small car.

When we finally loaded the car with our belongings, the vehicle was almost touching the ground. The whole scene seemed like it was right out of a comedy. With all of us in the Festiva, my mother's two dogs, our suitcases and bags, it looked very unlikely that we were going to make it 2000 miles. We all had a good laugh and never gave it a second thought. The Lord kept the car together. Thankfully, we only had a few scary moments. We had a good trip going down and have many stories to share for years to come.

One incident I remember in particular occurred when we were passing through Manitoba, heading to Saskatchewan. I told my mom I knew a short cut. I don't know what I was thinking, but it wasn't a short cut by any means. Instead of a six-hour trip, it lasted ten hours! It seemed like the road we were on would never end! After a long time, I had no idea where we were. We had been driving all night and each nameless town turned into another nameless one. We needed gas and we needed it soon. Finally, it was daybreak and we had come upon a town with a gas station but, to our disappointment, it was closed! Mom suggested we stay and wait, but I was confident that there was another town ahead. So after some discussion we went ahead. But all we saw was just more flat lands. I now understand the joke about seeing a dog running for days.

We were tired and exhausted and just wanted to see a town. Then we saw a hill. I was sure there was a little town just over the hill and as we were heading up the hill, we ran out of gas. We had to get out and push ourselves up the rest of the way. Once we got to the top, we found that there wasn't a town in site! We decided that we would head to a house we had passed about a kilometer back. We rolled down the hill and I, miserably, had to be the one to go the house at 5:00 a.m. and wake up whoever was inside sleeping. Just before leaving for the house, we saw a truck coming down the road. Thankfully, he stopped. It was a young man. Unfortunately, he didn't know much of the area either and he wasn't able to help us and so he went on his way.

As I approached the house, I began praying that there were no dogs on the property and that the people sleeping wouldn't be too upset with me when I woke them up. Only after I had awoken them and gotten them out of their bed did I notice the man with the truck had come back. I went over to see him and sure enough, this man had gotten some gas and said he had to live up to his license plates which read, "Friendly Manitoba". I suppose he had to leave a lasting impression of his province since we were now on Saskatchewan soil.

I went back to the house to apologize for my rude awakening and left. Then we were on our way again. I definitely feel for anyone who gets lost in the Saskatchewan plains.

These were times of stretching our patience for Mom and I. Being in such close quarters with each other was trying, but God was doing something in us, for us.

~nineteen~

The Loss of All Things

Isaiah 55:8-9

For my thoughts are not your thoughts, neither are your ways my ways, saith the LORD. For as the heavens are higher than the earth, so are my ways higher than your ways, and my thoughts than your thoughts.

When we finally arrived, we were informed that *Kokum* had been transferred to a hospital in Regina, Saskatchewan. This was almost a two hour drive away. I knew that this meant her condition was critical. *Kokum* had suffered a stroke and she had been placed on dialysis. It was heartbreaking. It was a real difficult time for all of us. It hurt so much to see her this way. We just wanted her to come back home. The trips in to see her were always hard and whenever she saw me, all she talked about was my wedding and how beautiful I would look as a bride.

She talked about the Saskatoon pies she was going to bake for our wedding. If only she could be there to witness my wedding and take part in it, but I knew the likelihood of her being there was slim.

One afternoon, she did something she had not done before; she called for my children one at a time and spoke with each of them. Sadly, I didn't know that this was going to be one of the last times I would have a chance to speak with her. I left my time of speaking with her for another day. Days earlier, the family had been informed by the doctors that she would have to be on the machines from now on. I had thought that this was going to happen. I anticipated that it was going to be a matter of adjusting and working things out. As long as *Kokum* would still be with us, I was happy.

A few days later, mom and I were having a conversation with a distant relative. I had driven in to visit *Kokum* at the hospital and was anxiously looking forward to my visit with her. What I heard my mom utter next made my heart sink! She told our relative that *Kokum* had been taken off the machines and that she had only a few days left to live. I couldn't believe what I had just heard! It was *Kokum's* wish that she didn't want a machine to keep her alive.

The next time I saw her, she had already been induced into a sleep. She had been heavily medicated now and the chances of her ever waking up again were unlikely. My opportunity to say goodbye was gone! My heart ached with the realization that *Kokum* had said her goodbyes to my children, and I had stood by oblivious to what was going on. I had missed my chance. I was devastated.

Had she been waiting for my farewell? Had I missed my chance to say good-bye? My heart was in anguish and it was so painful, I wasn't ready to say goodbye…all I could do was watch her sleep.

I feel her warmth as I run my fingers through her hair. I will kiss her one last time. "Can you hear me Kokum? Are the angels ministering to you…or are you with Jesus? Can you hear the angels sing?"

She was sleeping, so peacefully. I kissed her cheek and I only wanted to hold her once more. I tried to remember my last words with her; did I tell her how much I loved her? Would she know when I got married? With tears running down my face and my heart in pieces, I told her once more, *Kokum, I love you.*

I don't know who did it, but somebody suggested that Rick and I should get married by her bedside. We decided that if the finances became available we would do it – we would get married by *Kokum's* bedside. But we had no money and there were only days left. I wanted so much for *Kokum* to witness my wedding before she passed on. But, the prospect of this happening was practically next to none. *"Where was the money going to come from?"*

Neither of us had any money. We were so broke at the time that I remember my daughter Hasslina had asked for a drink. I knew we didn't have enough money to even get a drink. But I decided that I would call my bank just to see if I had enough to swipe my debit card to buy her a drink. When I called, I couldn't believe what I heard. I had over $1600.00 in my account! I didn't question it, instead I went to the machine to try and withdraw $100.00. Unbelievably, out came $100.00. Rick was on his way to the hospital and when he arrived, he had a hard time believing it as well. I had no idea where the money came from. This was a blessing! *(I found out later that it was child support arrears, although this hardly was ever on time, I wasn't expecting it.)* With the money in hand, we went ahead and got our marriage license and our rings. I went into prayer and asked the Lord to keep *Kokum* alive so she could witness this special event in my life.

The Wedding Day, August 10, 2005

My stepson-to-be called his pastor, knowing that if he could come he would. The pastor was a busy man and was on the road a lot. Rick came back with the good news; the pastor was available and he had agreed to marry us by *Kokum's* bedside.

Less than five minutes into our wedding ceremony, *Kokum* took her last breath. She was gone. I can still hear my mothers cry beside me as my vows were being read. When our wedding ceremony finished, instead of embracing my husband, I bent forward to hold my *Kokum*, to let out my tears...my heart ached and I wept.

My dearest and closest cousin embraced me and told me, "*Kokum* waited for you; she watched you while she was leaving." Tears streamed down my face. I knew *Kokum* saw us. My mom phoned my aunt to share the news of our wedding, and the death of *Kokum*. My aunt's response to our marriage union was unexpected. My mom was taken aback by my aunt's anger. I remember my mom describing her response as "icy." Neither of us understood why.

Married and Living on the Reserve...

Rick and I went back to the reserve. Our future together seemed bright. Rick was to be ordained and become an assistant pastor in my family's church. I was looking forward to ministering alongside of him. Instead, we quickly found out that doors we thought were open were now closing on us. We went to my family's church and he was publicly rejected. They announced that they would be looking for a new assistant pastor. Unbelievably, my husband's upcoming ordination had been withdrawn. It was a sad time for us and I knew my husband was discouraged by this, but he just reached out and held my hand.

It was evident that my family was angry that Rick and I had gotten married. I could sense that their behaviour toward me had changed since they had travelled out east together and I had come back from Ontario. Perhaps Rick had mentioned that I would not stand with them in the preaching of the prosperity message. Whatever it was, I don't know what had changed. We had now been cast aside. In time maybe they would come and see us. We are family and all one body in Christ, *right?*

Mark 6:11
"And whosoever shall not receive you, nor hear you, when ye depart thence, shake off the dust under your feet for a testimony against them."

We had to press in and fight the fight of faith. I knew that all things would work out, eventually.

The Funeral

I can vaguely recall the days following my *Kokum's* death. Had my *Kokum* prepared her funeral beforehand, I know that she would have ensured that I had a seat with the immediate family by her casket. *Kokum* had helped to raise three of her grandkids, including myself. Anyone who knew her knew how much she loved me. And they knew how much I loved her. They all had their seats close to her and, unfortunately, I wasn't there. This hurt so much – it hurt beyond words – but I thank the Lord He was with me. I remember leaving the wake to go and talk with the Lord.

"*Lord, you have to hold me together here. Don't let me fall apart!*"

It would be an understatement to say that emotions were running high in the days before and after

Kokum's passing. A lot of unnecessary things were said that hurt. I was criticized for what my children wore and so on. It was a sad and painful time. Everyone was grieving in their own way and I understood this. It was only the grace of God that helped me pull through.

On the day of her burial something wonderful happened that lifted my heart.

Kokum had wanted to be buried on her property next to her home. When the time came for the burial and we were on our way, we heard something above the noise of all the vehicles in the funeral procession. It was the sound of hundreds of wild horses! To see them is not an everyday occurrence. One could go a lifetime and never see these wonderful wild creatures. Their hoof beats thundered across the plain. They ran in the same direction we were headed. Amazingly, they weaved through the procession to pass us. All we could do was watch and be amazed and awed at this incredibly majestic display. My husband and I were in disbelief and awe. And then, as we approached the last stretch of the road before *Kokum's* final resting place, we saw the cattle.

Since I was a little girl, I could always remember the cattle that grazed there and on this day as we were passing, they started to run together in the same majestic display. It was beautiful and I knew it was the Lord's way to assure us that she was with Him in glory. I knew she was with the Lord in heaven now.

Life on the reserve was good for awhile. My husband and I would sit outside by the bonfire, play the guitar, and sing songs to the Lord. He loved to hunt and I would soon learn how to.

I was a city girl, an "urban Indian", and I soon learned that having my name brand coffee and store-bought meat was a real luxury when you live on the reservation. That was all left behind and here I was now, spotting for deer in the bushes. The next deer we saw was going to be dinner! I had to laugh; it was all so odd to me. I didn't even know the difference between an elk, a moose, or a deer. My husband shared a lot of his hunting stories with me, some hilarious and some daring. I was yet to see him in action. I teased him and we had lots of fun. We still bought our meat at the grocery store, but many of our people still eat wild meat. I was going to attempt to try it whenever the time came.

One evening, we decided to go out hunting and I figured it was for only sightseeing anyway. I didn't expect us to get anything. Hassan and my brother Shaun came along for the ride. Shortly after we got started, that's when we saw it. It was an elk. At first I had thought that it was a moose. It was massive. My husband took aim and fired. When I saw the elk go down, I couldn't believe it. My husband told me to phone our neighbor to round up a truck. He was going to need help. I left them there and was back within an hour. When I came back, my husband already had the elk skinned. I thought I was going to fall over from the smell! The whole gory and gruesome scene affected me immensely. Above all of this, all I could think of was the elk's family. He had come out for a bite to eat and now my husband wanted me to eat this beautiful elk! I had thought that when the time came that I would be up for eating wild meat. Now here it was in front of me and I couldn't do it. My husband had to take it in to a butcher shop to have it butchered and delivered to be eaten elsewhere.

With ministry doors closed, we decided to head to Alberta. My mom had called and she said she would come with me. The kids and I were going to go ahead to look for a place while my husband finished his contract up in the reserve. As Thanksgiving passed by, we left the reserve and headed to Alberta.

~twenty~

Rejected. Why Lord?

1 Corinthians 4:5
Therefore judge nothing before the time, until the Lord come, who both will bring to light the hidden things of darkness, and will make manifest the counsels of the hearts: and then shall every man have praise of God.

My husband finally made it over to Alberta and things were good for awhile. The Lord was opening doors for us and then, in just a short time, our life changed. All the things we had hoped for, the plans we had had for our marriage, were brought to a halt. My husband began to withdraw and things began surfacing. I wasn't sure what was happening, but I knew in my heart, something serious was coming. I brought our marriage before the Lord — repeatedly — believing and praying our marriage would survive.

One morning, after my husband went to work, I called a wonderful friend. She was an elder and mother in the Lord. She'd been established in ministry for years at Camp Living Water where many First Nation children had come to the Lord. I shared my burden with her and we went into prayer. When we were finished, she had a Word for me, saying that no weapon formed against me shall prosper. I remembered the last time I had quoted this scripture was during a difficult time. I knew then that things ahead were going to become more difficult.

Later that evening, as I lay down to read, I came across a passage of scripture from Isaiah 54:1 in the book I was reading at that time. The Spirit of the Lord began to move upon me. I knew the Lord was going to minister to my heart. As I read, tears filled my eyes. The Lord was holding me.

Isaiah 54:4-6, 14-15

Fear not; for thou shalt not be ashamed: neither be thou confounded; for thou shalt not be put to shame: for thou shalt forget the shame of thy youth, and shalt not remember the reproach of thy widowhood any more. For thy Maker is thine husband; the LORD of hosts is his name; and thy Redeemer the Holy One of Israel; The God of the whole earth shall he be called. For the LORD hath called thee as a woman forsaken and grieved in spirit, and a wife of youth, when thou wast refused, saith thy God.

In righteousness shalt thou be established: thou shalt be far from oppression; for thou shalt not fear: and from terror; for it shall not come near thee. Behold, they shall surely gather together, but not by me: whosoever shall gather together against thee shall fall for thy sake.

Tears streamed down my face. I knew Jesus was feeling my pain — my rejection — and it didn't matter what came against me, He was doing something. I knew the Lord had plans even for me. When my eyes landed on the next couple of scriptures, assurance and confidence filled my heart.

Isaiah 54:16-17
Behold, I have created the smith that bloweth the coals in the fire, and that bringeth forth an instrument for his work; and I have created the waster to destroy. No weapon that is formed against thee shall prosper; and every tongue that shall rise against thee in judgment thou shalt condemn. This is the heritage of the servants of the LORD, and their righteousness is of me, saith the LORD. {emphasis added}

I didn't know what was going to happen. I had to continue to trust my Father. Nothing made any sense to me and whatever was happening was bigger than Rick and I. My marriage, my life, and my children were in the Lord's hand and He had a plan and purpose. I could feel the Lord embrace me and I knew I wasn't alone. But I could feel the depth of the valley I was descending into. I knew that I was going to be spending a lot of time on my knees in prayer for God's grace to get through what lay ahead.

In a short time, my husband and I separated. He got a place an hour east of us. My pastor from church had agreed to counsel, but Rick never went. The times we spoke were becoming more seldom and our marriage was suffering.

March 1, 2006, was the last time I embraced my husband.

Towards the end of March, my mother and I decided to go visit my brother in Saskatchewan. It was awhile since we had last visited him and we were anxious to see my little nephew. My brother Shaun, my mom's second eldest, had moved out west before I had by a couple of years. Shaun, who was one for getting into problems with the law, had straightened out his life for the better. He was doing really well. He had met a wonderful girl, gotten married, and had a beautiful baby boy. I was excited and happy to be closer to him. We had always been close and I looked forward to getting acquainted with him again. We had children now and it was a real blessing to watch our children play with one another. Shaun's wife and I hit it off immediately. Our visit with them was good.

My brother was at a standstill with his current job and wanted a change so they decided to try things out in Alberta. The west was prospering and it seemed like the best thing to do and we were all happy about the decision. I was thankful to the Lord for giving us this time and bringing us together.

Mom and I decided to bring my nephew back with us to Alberta so that Shaun and his wife could tie things up for their move. Before we could head out however, my brother wanted to exchange the car seat that my mother had purchased for her grandson. So we headed to the mall to exchange it.

March 22, 2006

As we pulled up in front of the mall entrance, I thought I saw my husband go in through the front doors with a woman. I assumed it was his sister. I asked my brother to go and see if it was him while I parked the vehicle. I met my brother inside and he quickly confirmed that it was my husband and told me that he had spoken with him.

Now it was my turn to find him and talk to him. I was excited and nervous because it had been awhile since we had talked and I had been waiting to hear from him. It had been a couple of weeks since we were last together. I was sincerely hoping for the best between us.

When I finally found him I tried to shake the bad feeling I was getting from the woman he was with. When he came over to talk with me he made no attempt for introductions between her and I. Finally, I just asked who she was and he casually stepped back and put his arms around her and introduced her. My heart sank when I heard her name – she was his former girlfriend. I didn't know what to say or do, but I heard myself asking him, "Are you back together?" They both nodded. I turned and walked away. I couldn't believe this was happening to me.

What could I say? What could I do? This was my husband? He was still in love with her... He didn't know this before? How could he do this to me, or to her? Our vows to the Lord meant nothing to him? I was distraught and confused. Why was this happening to me? How naive I was to marry a man I thought I knew...Oh God!

I couldn't believe it! Why, of all places, did I have to run into him here on this day!? The timing for this couldn't have come at a worse time. It was just one day before I was to speak in Leslieville, Alberta. I was scheduled to share my testimony for Camp Living Water. How would I be able to do this?

We returned to my brother's place and finished loading up the truck. I told my mom what had happened. I was so hurt. I just wanted to get out of Saskatchewan as quickly as possible. As soon as we were on the road, I remember sitting in the truck and thinking that I wanted to run somewhere and yell, "*Why God? How could this be happening to me? Why? Why? Why?! What did I do?!*" I wanted to cry and scream, but I was stuck in a truck packed full of kids and my mom. As we drove, my heart broken before the Lord, my mom ministered to me saying, "Sonia, the enemy knows you're going to be testifying tomorrow and is trying to stop you." I continued in prayer before the Lord in silence. I didn't want to fall apart; not here, not now. Not in front of my children. "*Lord, strengthen me. Please come to me.*"

It felt like all of hell was coming against me. Yet, despite what my circumstances looked like, I knew in my heart that God was still in control. And no matter what, I was going to do something for His glory. I knew all I had to do was to just continue to trust Him. I loved my husband and I had to stay focused on the Lord and not on the given circumstances. I said, "*Lord I'm going all the way with you, no matter what happens.*"

Leslieville, Alberta, March 23, 2005

What were others going to think? I had to stay focused on Christ and not on my circumstance. My mind was bombarded with thoughts which could have crippled me if I allowed them to. I knew I had to go speak. The Lord was doing something in the midst of the surrounding storm – I just had to be obedient.

I remember feeling so nervous when it came time to speak the next day. *Oh, how am I going to do this?* Everything in me wanted to run out of that place. I became so nervous looking at all those people. My stomach was in knots and my body was perspiring. All hell was raging against my mind. I needed some time alone with the Lord and to just be alone, away from everyone. I needed to calm myself down. The only solace I could find was in a washroom. In that little cubicle, totally at the end of myself, I surrendered to His will. Nothing else mattered at this point except what he wanted. Knowing I was in my Heavenly Father's hand, I cried, *"Lord by obedience I will go. Give me your words to say. Help me Lord!"*

I went back to the table and felt led to open my bible to the first chapter of Jeremiah. It reminded me that Christ knew me even before I was born. It reminded me that there was a calling and a purpose in my life. As I read the scripture, the Spirit of the Lord began to minister to me.

> **Jeremiah 1:7-8**
> **But the LORD said unto me, Say not, I am a child: for thou shalt go to all that I shall send thee, and whatsoever I command thee thou shalt speak. Be not afraid of their faces: for I am with thee to deliver thee, saith the LORD.**

As I read, I felt the Lord's amazing presence surround and fill me. In an instant, my nervousness and fear all went away. God was faithful. When everything in me wanted to run out of that place, He comforted me and gave me the words to speak. I learned, and experienced firsthand, the powerful scripture that says, "When I am weak, He is made strong" (2 Corinthians 12:10). Christ was leading me into an area that grieved His heart in order to bring me into a place He loved. He led me out of the ruins. When I felt like I wasn't going to make it, Christ was with me every step of the way.

Isaiah 43:2
When thou passest through the waters, I will be with thee; and through the rivers, they shall not overflow thee: when thou walkest through the fire, thou shalt not be burned; neither shall the flame kindle upon thee.

Times at home were difficult. The Lord knew my heart that when I married it was going to be for life. I felt marred and discarded. In my prayer closet and weeping before the Lord, I cried and asked many questions, *"Why? How could I marry this man? Why didn't you close that door? Did I hear you wrong? How could this have happened?"* Every hindering thought came against my mind. Despite the many questions, I had to trust the Lord.

I thought of Gethsemane, before Christ was crucified. The enemy came to hurl insults at Him and hissed lies to sway Him from truth. Lies to thwart Him from doing God's will. Likewise, whenever we are in a terrible situation, it's hard to understand the purposes of God. Instead, we tend to listen to the lies that tell us that somehow we have missed the mark. When the voices come to assault and wound, this is the time we must stand on the Word of God. He always has a purpose and although we don't completely understand His purposes, He does. We just need to remember that we are in His hands. The only power that is given to the enemy is what the Lord allows (John 19:11).

Colossians 1:16
For by him were all things created, that are in heaven, and that are in earth, visible and invisible, whether they be thrones, or dominions, or principalities, or powers: all things were created by him, and for him:

I knew His ways and His thoughts were higher than mine.

I received news a short time later that my husband was saying disheartening things about me and this broke my heart even more. After the initial shock of it all, I wanted to lash out and say some horrible things back. Then I heard through family that he was now engaged — and still out there ministering!?

Where were the leaders? Why weren't they putting a stop to this? The leaders were that of my own family. But how could they say anything when their own marriage was established on the same foundation? I could only ask myself, 'What kind of testimony is this bringing to the Lord? A married man, engaged to another woman, and still in the ministry!?' Lord, have mercy on us!

I knew that what was happening in my family's church, and in my marriage, was not going unseen. In due time, all things would be judged. I knew I was not going to lean on my own understanding. God was on the move. The Lord was working on restoring and bringing to light those things that were hidden in darkness. He was doing it, in His mercy, for our benefit.

The voices that came could have destroyed me if it wasn't for the grace of God. All I could hear was the enemy's voice taunting me, "*You don't hear from God. Who are you anyway? Your ministry for God is over! What kind of testimony are you? No one desires you, not even your husband. Look at you now!*"

I knew there were going to be voices that rose against me to condemn me. Especially from those who carried the letter of the law.

2 Corinthians 3:6
Who also hath made us able ministers of the new testament; not of the letter, but of the spirit: for the letter killeth, but the spirit giveth life.

I knew the religious crowds would be first in line to judge and condemn me, but it didn't matter, it was the Spirit of God that gave me life. It didn't matter what people thought, it mattered what the Lord thought. He is the witness of the things that happened and were happening.

The valley I was in hurt. Yet Christ in His faithfulness ministered to my heart. He has opened doors that no man can shut. I felt in my spirit that He was assuring me that He would open many doors and that through these events many more lives would be touched. What this meant I wasn't sure.

I feared for my husband because he wasn't in the right place. My heart's cry for him unto the Lord was for Him to be merciful. I had made a vow before the Lord, a vow made from my heart. Rick was still my husband and I was still his wife. Was I now going to become a divorce statistic? The days ahead were going to be trying, but His faithfulness was beyond comprehension. Living my life from day to day meant going into my prayer closet daily. The choice was before me; was I going to sink or swim?

~twenty-one~

Blessing in the Storm

John 14:13
And whatsoever ye shall ask in my name, that will I do, that the Father may be glorified in the Son.

In the course of a few months of my wedding day, the kids and I were alone again. The whole ordeal shook me to the core.

I got a job at a grocery store. The pay was barely enough for the kids and I to survive on, but I continued to trust the Lord and spent much time in prayer. I had my church family and had met some wonderful people in the Lord. I was amazed by the Christian people the Lord was bringing into my life. Even my neighbours were Christians and they went to my church as well. They were God's gift to me during this difficult time.

Just days before Christmas, I needed to do some shopping and the car was not in good running condition. Without a car, I would not be able to shop and Christmas would be spoiled for us. I was running out of options and I didn't know what I was going to do. As I shared this burden with my neighbours they offered me the use of their car. I couldn't have imagined that they would do this. This was the Lord's favour! Because of their generosity the children and I had a wonderful Christmas.

I knew we had to get a vehicle soon. It was just a few weeks before, in fact, that mom and I had taken the little Festiva into Red Deer to get looked over by a mechanic. We were going to see about getting winter tires put on. When the mechanic came back to us he told us that the car wasn't worth fixing! He had us sign a waiver before we could leave; they weren't going to be responsible if something should happen to us. We had been dangerously driving an unfit vehicle! We signed the waiver and prayed over the vehicle to get us home. We knew instinctively that there had to have been angels holding that car together.

Though our circumstances seemed bleak, the Lord was moving and drawing my mother and I closer together. We were now joined together in prayer before the Lord where we were once far apart.

My mother worked as a Camp Attendant for the oilrigs and was away a lot. On her days off from work she would come over to my place. My mother was a big support for me. I couldn't have made it through without her. The Lord in His sovereignty was continuing to restore us in the midst of everything that was happening. Our relationship was stronger now. Our walk with the Lord was becoming deeper and our faith in Christ increased while we were learning to decrease. The Lord, through this difficult time, was continually refining and rebuilding us. My mother also helped to purchase another vehicle for us. Another amazing couple in the Lord also helped me to get insurance and clear other expenses. I was happy. We had a vehicle again, minus the oil and gas leak. I was encouraged by my mom to start praying over my vehicle. I knew this was what my mom always did and so I was going to do the same thing. Things were good. The Lord was good. But now I was beginning to face a new enemy, a new barrier.

My church was comprised of mainly Caucasians – white folks – and I stuck out like a sore thumb. Although they never meant to be rude I could perceive that I was not being received wholeheartedly. I had never experienced racism until I moved to western Canada. The Word of God tells us that we are one body in Christ, but to the community and, sadly, to this community of "believers," I was an Indian. Unfortunately, native people have been negatively stereotyped and labeled. In the mind of these people, I guess, I was just another Indian. No matter what anyone else believed, Jesus died for First Nations' people too and He loves us the same. God's Word holds hope and a promise for me as much as them. I just had to continue to press on, despite their attitudes toward me as a First Nations woman.

One day at work, an older Native woman came through the check-out and we hit it off right away. We exchanged numbers and I called her within a few days. I found out her daughter actually attended the same church I did! I was even more blessed when I found out she served the Lord too, but the best was yet to come when she told me she was praying for me. She had been praying that when people saw me that they would see more than what they saw. I couldn't believe what she said and I took this as confirmation that the Lord was going to open doors for residential cleaning for me. I had been praying about letting my job go so I could do residential cleaning. I knew it paid more and it would help us out, but I was afraid of rejection. I placed an ad in the newspaper and I was amazed at what the Lord provided. Wow! Doors opened, the work came, and I was even paid more than what I was asking for! I came across some amazing people who brought me into their own homes and blessed me.

No one rejected me, but one woman asked me in my first interview if anyone had turned me away after seeing me? I answered her "No, I haven't been turned away and I am very thankful that no one has; I don't think I could have handled that." I ended up working for this woman. The Lord had given me favour. Unfortunately, during my shopping and errands I encountered many people who just weren't very nice. I was getting a little taste of what some of our First Nations people endure on a daily basis. It wasn't a nice feeling and I began to understand why many of our First Nations people held onto their bitterness and hatred. I knew that many of my people needed healing in their hearts. I knew that what the Lord was seeing happening to our people was breaking His heart. Nonetheless, the racism and prejudices I was encountering only made it clear to me that the Lord had a blessing coming. I just needed to endure.

It was a day or so after Mother's Day when a woman I worked for called and asked to see me that evening. She told me she had something – a gift – for me. I was thrilled. Mother's Day had just passed and it touched my heart. She had thought about me. No one ever had before.

She called back and cancelled until the following day, my gift was not ready. I was definitely now very curious as to what this gift could be. I told her that I wasn't going to be able to sleep with all the suspense. As much as I pressed her to tell me what it was, she never relented. She never gave me one clue about the gift she had in store for me. I had no choice but to wait. After a sleepless night of wondering what it could be, I saw her pull up in my drive-way. I went out to meet her and she told me to jump in; my gift was at her house. Off we went.

I continued rambling on in the car until we pulled into her driveway. I noticed her expression had changed and I said, "*What?*" She motioned and I turned. There beside me was a van. Was she for real? I heard her ask, "Do you like it?" I was speechless. I didn't know what to say. The only thought that ran through my mind was "*No way! This isn't really happening*." I couldn't believe it. Who gives away vehicles? You hear about it happening to other people but never imagine it happening to you. She offered to drive me home while her husband followed us in my "new" van.

As we pulled up to my home, I ran in to tell my brother and sister-in-law, who had been waiting for me at home, that my gift was on the way and to come outside. I didn't say a word to them; I wanted to surprise them too. A moment later, her husband pulled into the driveway with my van. "There it is," I proclaimed. I looked at my sister-in-law's face and her mouth literally dropped open. Then my son who had been riding his bike rode up and asked "Where is it?" He had been anxiously waiting too, but never guessed it was right in front of him!

We were all overjoyed and thankful. I knew we were going to remember this day for a very long time.

I think I floated around for a couple of days. Then one day as I was driving into Red Deer, that's when it actually hit me. I just cried and said, 'Jesus you blessed me with a van.' An overwhelming sense of great awe of God filled my inner being. I was so overjoyed! It was the miracle I needed. With my husband gone and being rejected by him, this was a huge encouragement! It was God reaffirming things in our lives that He was going to take care of us.

Although satan wanted to destroy us, God was going to turn it for His good. The days ahead seemed bleak, but I had to learn to take it one day at a time. Trusting the Lord is all that I had, and it was everything I needed.

~twenty-two~

Where are Your People?

Genesis 50:20
But as for you, ye thought evil against me; but God meant it unto good, to bring to pass, as it is this day, to save much people alive.

A few years before, I had had two dreams. In the first dream, I was in an auditorium and it was filled with men and women of all ages. I was asked to speak and when I arose to speak, I noticed some get up to leave while others stayed.

In the second, I dreamt I was speaking again. The difference was that the location was much bigger. It was a stadium and it was filled! When I was asked to speak, the same thing happened, I could hear the chairs being moved and people leaving, I asked my uncle what this meant and he told me when the Lord begins to use me, I was going to lose family and friends.

Ironically, he was the first to walk away when my husband and I were married. It was just a short time later that a dear sister in the Lord did the same thing.

When I first moved out to Saskatchewan, I met a wonderful couple in the Lord who had also attended my family's church. When my husband and I moved out to Alberta, we lost touch. We all became close friends and I loved them dearly. I was very happy to finally get in touch with them again. I was sure now that there would be more intercessors in prayer for my marriage. They were nearby so we arranged for them to come visit us in Eckville, Alberta, the following weekend. Their visit would also happen to fall on my birthday. A few days before my birthday, however, I received a phone call from her husband. I thought he was phoning for directions, but what he said caused my heart to sink.

He told me they couldn't come. I asked him "Why?" I knew when he started talking to me something wasn't right. I thought that maybe other engagements had come up. Instead, he said, "It was nice meeting you again, but now it's time to go our separate ways. It is not the Lord's will that we be a part of your life. You need deliverance. You're not 'living right.'"

I didn't even know what to say. I couldn't believe what I was hearing! Then I heard myself ask him, "Is this what the body of Christ does?" He didn't say anything more but said goodbye. I hung up and went into my room to kneel before the Lord. My dreams were coming to pass, and I was feeling the sting of betrayal again. I knew something had been said to them to cause this to happen. Yet I knew in my heart that the Lord did not want me to say a thing. The Lord was my Defender. All I needed to do was to pray and forgive them.

Rejected again, I immersed myself in prayer. I still didn't understand anything, but I was going to seek answers. Something was terribly wrong here and I knew it grieved the heart of God.

Psalm 61:2-3
From the end of the earth will I cry unto thee, when my heart is overwhelmed: lead me to the rock that is higher than I. For thou hast been a shelter for me, and a strong tower from the enemy.

I went to work every day and pressed in to the presence of the Lord. No matter what happened I was going to continue to love the Lord with all my heart. I pressed on with my writing and focused on my children. They were doing well. They never cried for London and they seemed to settle in. My neighbour's children were close to the same age as mine were and they hit it off great! They were making friends.

We especially loved to go for drives into the mountains. We were close to Rocky Mountain House and Nordegg, Alberta. Both places were spectacular! We had some awesome times and I knew it was only God's grace that was helping me. There was strength and safety in His arms. I knew beyond the shadow of a doubt that if the world rejected me, He was still with me.

The raging storm that I witnessed in my dream before leaving Ontario wasn't going to overtake me. Though at times, its noisome winds made me afraid, I'd learned to draw into the Lord. We won't be consumed and the waters won't overtake us if we apply the Word and stay near the Father. "Keep your eyes off the circumstances, and keep your eyes on Me, you will make it through this storm!"

Then at the most perfect time, a woman from work spoke words of life to me when I really needed to hear them. When I arrived at work, she was there and I was so glad. I needed someone who would listen and that I could share my burdens with. I thank the Lord she was there. I told her that the very things the Lord had shown me while I was back in Ontario were now coming to pass and that I had walked right into them.

I was trying to grasp and understand the things that were happening because I was witnessing friends and different ones in the Lord begin to fall away. When I had come back to church, I knew there was something different about it. I saw a man who was in the worship group go out for a cigarette. Then I watched a pillar in the church fall and go right back into the bar scene. I could see that the enemy was creeping in with lies and deception. I couldn't understand how this was being allowed into our churches. How was this all happening?

And then I walked into the worst battle of my life. It was a battle I was unprepared for. There was no where else to go but to the Lord. I did not want the world and I sure wasn't going to run back to it. I was burdened with what was happening in some of our churches. I entered the prayer closet and the Lord began to open up His Word to me. The Lord began to show me things that were causing His heart to grieve. They were things that, if shared, would stir the waters. But these were things that He was showing me, things He was causing me to see and understand. I understood that He wanted me to speak up against these things. But how was I able to speak against family? How was I able to do this? I knew I had to. It was no longer a question; it was a matter of being obedient.

She listened and ministered to me by saying that the Lord was going to supersede over all things in my life. He was going to surpass many things that I couldn't even begin to imagine. Her words of encouragement were staggering! I knew her words were confirmed later when the Lord reminded me of where I had come from. It was His Spirit that was going to change the wayward hearts of His people; just like how He was changing mine.

I had seen Him over the course of that year deliver over and over again. He provided everything for me, including my dictionaries so I could write this book.

It happened on a beautiful Saturday morning. I was heading out to find some garage sales (one of my favourite pastimes). My brother Shaun came with me. I had told him that I was looking for a good dictionary, but the cost of a good one was too much. We eventually made it over to Rocky Mountain House; it wasn't that far, maybe a half hour drive away.

Thankfully, he found what he was looking for – a bike for his wife. As we were loading up the van, the man who was holding the garage sale came over to me and asked me if I wanted some dictionaries.

I could not believe what I had just heard, in fact, I still replay that moment over again in my mind when I'm in hard times. It reminds me that the Lord will always provide. I literally had been handed another tool to help me write this book. Although, I knew my book wouldn't be perfect and would not be written with the best of words, I knew that it would be written from my heart. Having this dictionary would help. I was even more blessed that as I searched for different words in the dictionaries I would often find Bible scriptures alongside its meaning. How much better could I have done? And how many dictionaries come with scripture nowadays? They were two encyclopedia dictionaries and they were the most beautiful books I ever laid eyes on. *Wow!*

I went home smiling and thanking the Lord. This was one of the first few instances that I could testify of the Lord's amazing provision for my life. Since my ex-husband had left, I was never in need. I continued to marvel at the Lord's wonderful care and concern for the littlest things in my life. I saw His hand even upon my home. The house that we had was subsidized and, although my husband had left me with the rent payments, we didn't lose our home. The vacancy rate in Alberta at the time was next to nil, so we were blessed.

I had everything to continue writing and I was set away from distractions. Eckville was a small town.

Once a week or so the kids and I would go into the city of Red Deer to watch a movie. Additionally, the family who blessed us with the van would give us gift certificates for dinner at different restaurants. The Lord's blessing through them toward us was unbelievable! The children, my mother, and I would have an awesome time dining at some really nice places. We did not have the chance to get out to nice restaurants often, so this was a definite treat!

With the Lord's provision in place, I knew I had to do what I was called to do. The Lord has a purpose for everything in our lives, no matter how big or how small. No matter what poor choices we make, the Lord is able to come and uplift you with His hand. He will use everything that happens for His glory! He is saying to the world, whatever is impossible with man is possible with Him. Everything is under His control. If I had listened to the condemning voices that said I was a failure, and that the Lord wasn't with me, I would have fallen.

The Lord was going to show me something else...

I had a wonderful experience happen to me as I was driving into work one morning. As I was driving and thinking about the things that had transpired over the course of a few months, the Lord reminded me of an answered prayer.

Days before *Kokum's* passing, I was worried and afraid *Kokum* wouldn't forgive and would die of a hardened heart. Days before her passing, my aunt and uncle went in to see her. I knew *Kokum* had been very disillusioned by the way my aunt and uncle had started their ministry. It had been borne out of an adulterous relationship and I knew this had grieved *Kokum*. I wondered if she would ever be able to forgive them for what they had done. *Kokum* had turned to my aunt and said the words that we were all waiting to hear. She had looked at her and said "I love you." This could only have been done as a result of an outpouring of God's love in *Kokum's* heart. God's love was evident and because of it we knew that *Kokum* was in God's heavenly glory. Tears flooded my eyes remembering this. What the enemy had wanted to destroy, the Lord had turned it all for His glory.

It's His love that covers all transgressions. His love is what He came to give the world. This is how the world will know that we are His disciples: if we love one another. This love, which men and women are searching for, is in God. He is the Lover of our souls and the only One who can make our hearts ablaze. God is love, and if you say you know Him, then you will love others, and this love will compel and draw others to Him.

John 13:34-35
"A new commandment I give unto you, That ye love one another; as I have loved you, that ye also love one another. By this shall all men know that ye are my disciples, if ye have love one to another."

An amazing outpouring of love swelled up for my family, I loved them all so much. But was I going to bow down to what they were doing? How could I? I just couldn't. This was my predicament and to speak out on the Lord's behalf was going to cost me. It already had. Yet I was not going to do this without fighting for my family. I determined to contend with my enemies in prayer.

My "enemies" were not of flesh and blood. My war wasn't with my family. I love my family including my former husband. My war lies with the deceitfulness of the heart, the sin that has hardened the heart. These were the spiritual enemies I would contend with. They were enemies from within. I had to remember as much as I loved them and wanted my family to like me, it was not up to me. Many have become blind. It is only the mercy of God that will shake and move what is not of Him to bring those who are blind and in error into a place of repentance.

I was reminded of a story about a man named Eli. He was a priest and judge over the Lord's temple and His ark. He had two sons who were vile. They possessed no reverence for the Lord. A prophet came to Eli and warned him about judgment if he did not restrain his two sons. Although warned, Eli continued to allow these grievous things to enter into God's house. His sons continued to practice perversion at the door of the temple. The Lord then used a child named Samuel to reach Eli. This young boy, who grew up in the tabernacle, spoke to Eli and told him that the judgments that were spoken against him by the prophet were going to happen soon.

Soon after, judgment fell on Eli's house. His two sons died in battle, and the Ark of the Covenant, which they had carried into the battle, was captured. When Eli heard the news he fell over and broke his neck. His daughter-in-law, Phinehas' wife, who was with child and now full of grief because of her loss, gave birth. She named her son *Ichabod*. Her son's name meant '*the Glory of the Lord has departed*.' After this she gave up and died (1 Samuel 2:12-4:22).

Was I too going to give up and die? Was I going to turn my ear from the truth that I was witnessing? No! I was not going to! The Lord wasn't going to allow me to die. He will use voices and raise them up to speak His Word. There will be men and women who love the Lord and who won't bow to compromise. The world is watching and I know there will not be any blood on my hands. There is a coming judgment for those who are taking God's grace and using it for their own gain and men who look to their own way. I knew that what I was witnessing was not of God. I could not and would not close my eyes to it.

Rise up my beloved!

It was during this time, I began to encourage myself in the Lord. I knew I was required to rise up. It was time to rise. This wasn't going to take me down. I was not going to die! Christ was going to continue to lead me out of this for His glory.

~twenty-three~

What is Happening in Your House?

Ezekiel 13:22
Because with lies ye have made the heart of the righteous sad, whom I have not made sad; and strengthened the hands of the wicked, that he should not return from his wicked way, by promising him life:

There weren't very many people who contacted me or stayed in touch with me during this whole ordeal. I did have two aunties who came out and visited me. My dad also came out to visit. This was nice and helped to encourage me. Not many others did. I know some were probably very confused and left wondering what had gone wrong.

This representation of Christ was a false representation. There was more to Him than what we were portraying. Christ Jesus, my Lord, my Savior, my

Healer, and my Friend meant so much more. I knew the Lord's heart felt grieved over this, and it hurt.

There are many reading this book that may face similar circumstances. To you I extend encouragement. No matter the circumstances that surround you press in to the presence of the Lord. I know there are others who are witnessing grievous things in the house of God, or perhaps been directly hurt by someone in the ministry. Just remember to keep your eyes on Jesus. Men and women fail and ministries will fall, but Christ wants our focus on Him, and Him alone. Although the assaults against the Church are increasing, the gates of hell will not prevail against the Church (Matthew 16:18).

How Lord? How do men and women who once loved you fall away? How does this happen? Help me to understand that I may minister life unto the hearers. Help me to open up this Word to other's who are confused or hurt.

The apostle Paul wept night and day for three years when he saw the coming deception that would creep into the church. His heart grieved over this age in which we now live.

Acts 20:29-31
For I know this, that after my departing shall grievous wolves enter in among you, not sparing the flock. Also of your own selves shall men arise, speaking perverse things, to draw away disciples after them. Therefore watch,

and remember, that by the space of three years I ceased not to warn every one night and day with tears.

Jesus, before He was to be crucified, turned to the women who were weeping for Him,

Luke 23:28
But Jesus turning unto them said, "Daughters of Jerusalem, weep not for me, but weep for yourselves, and for your children."

Christ Jesus knew of this hour when men and women would be deceived. There are pop culture celebrities who can perform "miracles" on TV. They claim to have the ability to walk on water and levitate. One in particular performs illusions that are so out of this world that people flock to him. More and more we are witnessing the rise of the supernatural, and we must not be swallowed up or fascinated by it. It is witchcraft. I first saw this young illusionist on TV and it gave me goose bumps to realize these same kinds of people are in our churches and are deceiving many. The Bible warns of such imposters, so let us not be ignorant.

2 Corinthians 11:14-15
And no marvel; for Satan himself is transformed into an angel of light. Therefore it is no great thing if his ministers also be transformed as the ministers of righteousness; whose end shall be according to their works.

In light of this scripture, it is no great thing then if satan's ministers masquerade as ministers of righteousness in our very midst. Their end reward, however, shall be according to their wicked works. We are in a day where our passivity towards these ministers of deception will cost us even our own salvation if we are not vigilant and discerning. Be warned and know this, that some of these very same illusionists will do signs and wonders and deceive many.

> **Matthew 24:24**
> **For there shall arise false Christs, and false prophets, and shall shew great signs and wonders; insomuch that, if it were possible, they shall deceive the very elect.**

How can we protect ourselves and not be deceived? The answer is in Jesus and keeping our eyes on Him. Think of Peter before Jesus was to be crucified. Peter denied Jesus three times and this was because Peter looked to men and to their faces. Peter was fearful of their faces because he took his eyes off of Jesus. We must learn from this story. This same thing can happen to us if we do the same. We must keep our eyes on Jesus. We must not look to man. As time goes on, those who love the Lord and refuse to compromise will be hated by all men.

Our guard has come down. Ungodliness is increasing and will only become worse. We have lost our passion for the things of the Lord and we need to repent and draw back to Him. If satan can continue to keep us out of our prayer closet, we lose our power.

Let us return unto the Lord and seek His forgiveness for allowing the busyness of our life to keep us from intimacy with Him. We need to remember from where He took us out of. We must repent and return to the Lord with all of our heart. I once heard a statement that rings true for a lot of us: *You can't shake a Mormon or a Jehovah's Witness, but a Christian will swallow anything*.

We become so self-absorbed that we lose our focus and our discernment.

1 Corinthians 10:12
Wherefore let him that thinketh he standeth take heed lest he fall.

Many are over-confident that they will not be deceived! This confidence is a confidence in the flesh. This is where we need to be cautious. Our confidence must be in Him and in His Word. We need to hold fast to the Word of God!

2 Timothy 2:15
Study to shew thyself approved unto God, a workman that needeth not to be ashamed, rightly dividing the word of truth.

I've heard many say they could never be deceived, but too many are swallowing everything they hear. Let us be diligent to be walking in the Spirit and not in our flesh. These are days that will only get harder. Men will be lovers of themselves and will take their position behind our pulpits. And sadly, they will lead many down a path of deception.

> **2 Timothy 3:1-4**
> **This know also, that in the last days perilous times shall come. For men shall be lovers of their own selves, covetous, boasters, proud, blasphemers, disobedient to parents, unthankful, unholy, without natural affection, trucebreakers, false accusers, incontinent, fierce, despisers of those that are good, traitors, heady, highminded, lovers of pleasures more than lovers of God;**

All this speaks of where we are today as a society. Ungodliness will continue to increase and the heart of man will wax worse.

I heard a woman speaking on one of the popular talk shows sharing her views. She was an atheist. She spoke defiantly against God. Her theology was that God was another Santa Claus and that He does not exist. But the most disturbing thing was the feedback she received from once believing Christians through email. Incredibly, many agreed with her! Pastors were leaving the ministry. Churches were becoming empty halls. Her argument was that God was used as a coping mechanism to get by. Thousands upon thousands believe this lie.

One of my closest friends back in London, whom I love with all my heart, shares the same view. She expressed to me the same thing; men and women use God because they can't stand on their own, and that this belief gets us by because we can't do things on our own.

My friend and her views are shared by many. I had to respect her and just love her. I know I will not win her by preaching to her. Instead, I talk to her like she knows what I'm talking about when it comes to spiritual matters, and I know she respects this. I love her and will continue to love her despite what she may feel. I know the words ministered unto her will not return void. It will be by my life, and the presence of Christ in my life, that will draw her into His presence and I leave her in His hands.

Whenever we neglect our prayer closet, the flesh will ever so subtly rear its ugly head. Our former man will rise and entangle us again. Satan and his distractions are deviously subtle. Before we know it, our time with the Lord decreases to the point where we have lost our power. Where we were once able to hear the voice of God, He has become a faint voice. His voice has become a dimming candle. When our ears have become dull of hearing, then it has become dangerous. Listen to the prophet Jeremiah, and to what Christ is saying;

Jeremiah 2:21-24
Yet I had planted thee a noble vine, wholly a right seed: how then art thou turned into the degenerate plant of a strange vine unto me? For though thou wash thee with nitre, and take thee much soap, yet thine iniquity is marked before me, saith the Lord GOD. How canst thou say, I am not polluted, I have not

gone after Baalim? see thy way in the valley, know what thou hast done: thou art a swift dromedary traversing her ways; A wild ass used to the wilderness, that snuffeth up the wind at her pleasure; in her occasion who can turn her away? all they that seek her will not weary themselves; in her month they shall find her.

This passage is referring to His children. They had once known Him and had now become a strange vine. *Why*? They had begun to allow the flesh to rule and dictate their lives. They had become indifferent to the things of God. They were running after the lust of the flesh. Whenever we stop yielding to the Spirit of God, in time, the flesh will win over. This is why ministers are being exposed more and more. Somehow they have begun believing the lie that their sin is ok. Somewhere along the way, they stopped yielding to the Holy Spirit.

The result is that we now have workers of iniquity who are driven by their lusts who were once strong believing servants. They have become blinded by their own lusts and can no longer discern truth from error. They have been given over to a rebellious heart and are under an illusion to believe the lie (2 Thessalonians 2:11).

1 Timothy 4:1
Now the Spirit speaketh expressly, that in the latter times some shall depart from the faith,

giving heed to seducing spirits, and doctrines of devils;

False doctrines are springing up everywhere and many are swallowing up their devilish deceptions. This is because many are not eating the Word and are spending less and less time in the prayer closet. It seems the messages we hear today are just "feel good messages." Repentance is seldom preached now.

In staggering proportions, these ministers have caused many to walk in error. These ministers have shut out the voice of God and no longer hear the truth of his Word. Instead of listening to the Lord's conviction they call those things that are evil good and good evil (Isaiah 5:20). This causes the sleeping Christian, who has stopped praying and meditating on the Word of God, to turn from truth and run to teachers who believe and teach a lie. If our heart is filled with greed, we'll run to hear and devour the messages of those who preach the prosperity message. And if we have sin in our lives, we will not sit under conviction, but instead, will run to teachers who also err from truth.

2 Timothy 4:3-4
For the time will come when they will not endure sound doctrine; but after their own lusts shall they heap to themselves teachers, having itching ears; and they shall turn away their ears from the truth, and shall be turned unto fables.

Their messages sound good, but it has no substance. When the storms come, it won't hold them. There is no substance and it is all works for the flesh. There are many doctrines – false doctrines – that are missing the mark. Many ministries are raised up for personal gain and profit in the Lord's name. This is abomination and it is grieving the heart of the Lord. I read the words of Jude and share with him in his burden. Sadly, this glorious gospel is being falsely represented, and those who fear His name must contend, steadfast, for the truth of His Word. The lives of many depend on our steadfast desire to bear the burden of truth for His name's sake. There are many who need hope and are searching.

Jude 1:3-4
Beloved, when I gave all diligence to write unto you of the common salvation, it was needful for me to write unto you, and exhort you that ye should earnestly contend for the faith which was once delivered unto the saints. For there are certain men crept in unawares, who were before of old ordained to this condemnation, ungodly men, turning the grace of our God into lasciviousness, and denying the only Lord God, and our Lord Jesus Christ.

~twenty-four~

"I Will Prosper You, but Don't Forget Me."

John 10:27

"My sheep hear my voice, and I know them, and they follow me:"

After being in Alberta for awhile, I wanted to come back to Saskatchewan. My mother had decided to move to Canora, Saskatchewan in order to be closer to her dad. And I wanted to be closer to my mom. I had been hoping to find my own place in Yorkton but it didn't work out that way. So I decided to move in with her. The house we shared was only a two bedroom house. It was cramped. Then the hot water tank stopped working. Mom was out in Alberta working at the time and I had to wait until she came home to settle the water issue. I wasn't getting anywhere with it. In the meantime, my dad suggested applying for a house with the Cowessess First Nation.

It was not an appealing thought to me. I really wasn't too anxious to move out there, but I was in a tough spot. I applied to the band office for a house under the social housing program. To my surprise, I got it!

John21:18
"Verily, verily, I say unto thee, When thou wast young, thou girdest thyself, and walkedst whither thou wouldest: but when thou shalt be old, thou shalt stretch forth thy hands, and another shall gird thee, and carry thee whither thou wouldest not." This spake he, signifying by what death he should glorify God. And when he had spoken this, he saith unto him, "Follow me."

I know the Lord will continue to restore, uproot, destroy, and pull down things that are not of Him. Then His people will see, that if we trust Him, as He has promised He will part the Red Sea in our lives.

Micah 7:15
According to the days of thy coming out of the land of Egypt will I shew unto him marvelous things.

The Lord is calling for repentance and hearts to turn back to Him. He desires His people to repent and to turn to Him. Once they do, we will see revival and healing in our land.

When I moved out to Cowessess, I remember days when fear would try to creep in and overwhelm me. Then I heard the Word ministered which greatly calmed me (2 Kings 6:8-17).

We hear a story of a king from Syria making war with Israel. He consults with his servants and makes his plan for victory. Elisha, a man of God for Israel, hears from the Lord about the enemy's plans. Elisha prays and the enemy's plans are thwarted. The king of Syria then wants to know if there is a traitor among them. They learn that Elisha is in Israel and he sends his men to find him. He sends his chariots and a great army at night, surrounding the city to capture Elisha.

> **2 Kings 6:15-17**
> **And when the servant of the man of God was risen early, and gone forth, behold, an host compassed the city both with horses and chariots. And his servant said unto him, Alas, my master! how shall we do? And he answered, Fear not: for they that be with us are more than they that be with them. And Elisha prayed, and said, LORD, I pray thee, open his eyes, that he may see. And the LORD opened the eyes of the young man; and he saw: and, behold, the mountain was full of horses and chariots of fire round about Elisha.**

Praise God, I know I'm not alone. I know that I can trust the Lord. Yes, even when the enemy is growling before us, remember Christ our Lord has already won the battle. We need to stand up and declare the Word! We have been given all that we need. We need to be diligent in training and becoming transformed daily. As Olympians that train for hours, days, months, and years, so should we also train and be prepared.

Jeremiah 1:6-10
Then said I, Ah, Lord GOD! behold, I cannot speak: for I am a child. But the LORD said unto me, Say not, I am a child: for thou shalt go to all that I shall send thee, and whatsoever I command thee thou shalt speak. Be not afraid of their faces: for I am with thee to deliver thee, saith the LORD. Then the LORD put forth his hand, and touched my mouth. And the LORD said unto me, Behold, I have put my words in thy mouth. See, I have this day set thee over the nations and over the kingdoms, to root out, and to pull down, and to destroy, and to throw down, to build, and to plant.

We need to look past the religious crowds and not give ear to the religious voices that seek to condemn and destroy us. Press in and look past all their faces and get past the fear of men (Proverbs 29:25).

No matter how charming they may seem, no matter how compelling the words they speak may be, or how highly educated someone might be, if it's not of the Holy Spirit, then it is not of God! The gospel of Christ has never changed. It is still the same. The simplicity of the gospel, and the answer for anyone searching, is found in the Cross of Calvary where Jesus Christ gave up His life for all sinners.

2 Corinthians 11:3
But I fear, lest by any means, as the serpent beguiled Eve through his subtilty, so your minds should be corrupted from the simplicity that is in Christ.

The Cross

The message of the Cross is seldom preached anymore, but it's the only way we'll have victory. Christ's only intent is that we be His hands and feet. If we do His will, we will abound in His Spirit with His power and His love. It is not difficult. It is simple obedience to His every Word. Take up thy cross and follow Him so we may do His, the Holy Spirit's, and our Father's will.

Galatians 2:20
I am crucified with Christ: nevertheless I live; yet not I, but Christ liveth in me: and the life which I now live in the flesh I live by the faith of the Son of God, who loved me, and gave himself for me.

Listen to the heart of Paul for a moment. Listen to how he wrestles as we all do. As we hear Paul's cries, may the Lord minister to our hearts that we cannot play with sin.

Romans 7:15, 24
For that which I do I allow not: for what I would, that do I not; but what I hate, that do I.

O wretched man that I am! who shall deliver me from the body of this death?

Romans 8:10-11
And if Christ be in you, the body is dead because of sin; but the Spirit is life because of righteousness. But if the Spirit of him that raised up Jesus from the dead dwell in you, he that raised up Christ from the dead shall also quicken your mortal bodies by his Spirit that dwelleth in you.

Our bodies are dead and in all of us, is sin. It is only through Jesus and what He has done that we are able to call ourselves heirs and His children. It is not by our works, lest a man should boast, but those who believe all have the same inheritance. He is not a respecter of persons (Acts 10:34). There is a wonderful New Covenant that we have. When Christ Jesus came and died, a blood covenant was made between God and His Son. It is a covenant that we may now enter into as heirs of the inheritance that Christ bought and redeemed for us through His life. We are promised to be partakers of every promise – of the entire inheritance – because of this New Covenant between the Father and His Son.

Our adversary knows of our victory and of the promises that have been given unto us, but his plan is to thwart you from getting into a place of standing on the promises of God. Sadly, many have been stopped and cut down by the attacks of the enemy. Today, many have fallen away.

Matthew 15:8
"This people draweth nigh unto me with their mouth, and honoureth me with their lips; but their heart is far from me."

In my short time walking with the Lord, I have heard of many sad things happening. I know of ministers who have fallen away and who have just given up. Perhaps the battle was too much for them. Somewhere along the way, they had grown passive and they quit fighting. In my own battles, I have wanted to quit — not on Jesus — but on going any further in ministry. Had I quit, this book would have gone unfinished. I would just like to take this time to encourage anyone in this situation now, to keep going and to press in. No matter the intensity, our life here is only but a vapour (James 4:14).

I battled often to get to the prayer closet, but once I was there, the Lord was faithful. Whenever I left my prayer closet, I came out strengthened and renewed. Whenever I don't make it into prayer, everyone around me knows; I become miserable. I need the prayer closet. His presence is the only place I draw strength from, and we need to continually enter into that rest. In prayer, He has ministered to my heart. He has moved me to tears. His love for us is so much and His only desire is that we love Him.

I remember talking to my sister and saying to her, "We're not going to follow Jesus because we have to; we will only do it, if we love Him." The only way to love someone is spending time and getting to know them. Loving Christ requires the same thing. As you draw near to Him, He will draw near to you. You will know His presence and His love will captivate you and move you. To all my brethren in the Lord, continue to walk with Him.

Christ wants us to abound; there are greater things than what we see. Satan's biggest ploy is the here and now, and it's working. His lies and ploys feed the lusts of our flesh. He deceives us into thinking that if our marriages are not working, we should get a new one. If it looks good, then buy it. If it feels good, then do it. It's all instant gratification and satisfaction. Take heed, Christ is thinking of your eternal salvation. Whatever the battle is, we're not alone. Remember, that there are many others who are enduring through the same battles.

> **1 Corinthians 10:13**
> **There hath no temptation taken you but such as is common to man: but God is faithful, who will not suffer you to be tempted above that ye are able; but will with the temptation also make a way to escape, that ye may be able to bear it.**

It is tragic and sad to watch as someone you love slips and falls away from the Lord. I've watched it time and time again. Many will quit the walk and get shipwrecked. We must endure for them, and for others, and be a light. Some have believed the deceptive lie that we are covered in grace and that it gives us the license to do whatever we want. This is not so! I'm referring to men and women who sin and refuse to turn from their sinful ways. God's grace is freely given if we are continually walking towards Him and our hearts are on Him. Though we may fall, He is always there to lift us up. Like the Father He is, He will take us by the hand. We must take heed to the Word of God for the sake of those who don't know the Word. For their sake's, we must draw near to the Lord. Our enemy is always at work to stop us from being a testimony unto others. Know this, you will be tested and be tossed about by hard times. Let me remind you again to listen to the heart of Paul and how he wept because he knew the coming hour of this day.

Our walk with the Lord requires prayer and staying diligent in seeking Him. Our God is not somewhere out in the galaxy watching us fall in ruin, but His eyes go to and fro throughout the world seeking a heart that will trust in Him. He is always at work. He is omniscient and omnipresent. He is the Alpha, and the Omega. He is the beginning and the end. And if we stay narrow minded, we will miss out on His plans for us. God is the Creator of our universe, and He breathed life into man. There are galaxies beyond number. The universe is so vast it is beyond the knowledge of all of our human scientists put together. Our salvation is in Him. Our hope is in Him. Our joy is in Him. Everything is in Him. To have it all, and then to lose it all, is not worth it. He has put our future and our promises in the Word, but we must go and find it. Even if we had the world at our feet, it would still not be enough! Just ask anyone with money; they know that something is still missing!

There was a certain rich man that came to Jesus and asked Him what he had to do to have eternal life. Christ Jesus told him in love to go and sell all that he had. He is the discerner of men's hearts and He knew this man's heart was focused on earthly possessions and not on God. This man lacked faith in God. His trust was in his riches. Christ tells us to build up our treasures in heaven:

Matthew 6:20-21
"But lay up for yourselves treasures in heaven, where neither moth nor rust doth corrupt, and where thieves do not break through nor steal: For where your treasure is, there will your heart be also."

The Lord can give us all things if He wanted to. It's all in His hands. Above all else, it is His will that He builds us up in order to strengthen us. He lays a foundation and removes things out of us that are not of Him. In time, we will grow and begin to understand. Just remember to live by faith and take it day by day.

Mark 10:21-22
Then Jesus beholding him loved him, and said unto him, "One thing thou lackest: go thy way, sell whatsoever thou hast, and give to the poor, and thou shalt have treasure in heaven: and come, take up the cross, and follow me."

And he was sad at that saying, and went away grieved: for he had great possessions.

Although many are building, sadly, it will all be for nothing. They are doing things by the works of the flesh and building for self. They are building up ministries all for gain and for their own glory, but there is a dreadful day coming. I write only to encourage that you draw in while His presence can still be found. He's the only one that can stir and change the heart.

One afternoon, while I was in my kitchen cooking, I was in worship. As the worship music played, the Lord stirred up this Word in my heart:

Ecclesiastes 9:11
I returned, and saw under the sun, that the race is not to the swift, nor the battle to the strong, neither yet bread to the wise, nor yet riches to men of understanding, nor yet favour to men of skill; but time and chance happeneth to them all.

I was so incredibly moved! His love for us is staggering and we miss it! His desire is to bless us and prosper us beyond means. But His greatest desire is that we stay close to Him. I knew that what the Lord was saying to me was, "*Yes, Sonia, I will prosper you, but don't forget me.*"

He loves us all so much. We must not let anything else steal Him from our hearts — especially sin. So many are using His name for profit and are denying

His power. By this I mean, they are not allowing Him to move, instead they are using the flesh to generate emotional responses. It has to be Him and the savour of Christ. We are commanded to test every spirit.

1 John 4:1
Beloved, believe not every spirit, but try the spirits whether they are of God: because many false prophets are gone out into the world.

I pray to the Lord that everyone who reads these words may keep them. If there is only one thing that you digest throughout the course of reading this book, my hope is that it is this: *that you know the importance of testing and trying the spirits.* Draw near to the Lord and He will direct you. I was so naive before. I know that there are many who are in similar circumstances as I was. I know there are many who are young in the Lord who may be easily deceived. My words are intended to build and edify you with love. In all your ways acknowledge Him. There will be many on that day that will appear before the Lord and believe they will enter heaven's gate, but many will be turned away.

Matthew 7:21-23
"Not every one that saith unto me, Lord, Lord, shall enter into the kingdom of heaven; but he that doeth the will of my Father which is in heaven. Many will say to me in that day, Lord, Lord, have we not prophesied in thy name? and in thy name have cast out devils? and in

thy name done many wonderful works? And then will I profess unto them, I never knew you: depart from me, ye that work iniquity.”

~twenty-five~

His Eyes are on You

Psalm 27:3-4
Though an host should encamp against me, my heart shall not fear: though war should rise against me, in this will I be confident. One thing have I desired of the LORD, that will I seek after; that I may dwell in the house of the LORD all the days of my life, to behold the beauty of the LORD, and to enquire in his temple.

I can't wait until that day, when we're in the presence of the glory of the Lord. I can't wait to see the look of my children's faces when they see the Lord. What a day that will be!

I know that there are many lovers of Jesus who are rising now and taking position. Men and women of God who are in love with Him are being placed on the battlefield to stand for the Lord and His truth.

In the hour you think you are alone, and think that you are the only one standing for truth, (because you will stand alone at times) be confident in knowing that you are not alone – He is with you always.

There is a powerful illustration of this in 1 Kings 19:1-18.

Jezebel was angry with Elijah and wanted him dead. Elijah went and slept under a juniper tree and requested for himself that he may die. He said,

1 Kings 19:4
It is enough; now, O LORD, take away my life; for I am not better than my fathers.

Then as he lay and slept under the juniper tree, an angel touched him, and said unto him, "Arise and eat."

1 Kings 19:10
And he said, I have been very jealous for the LORD God of hosts: for the children of Israel have forsaken thy covenant, thrown down thine altars, and slain thy prophets with the sword; and I, even I only, am left; and they seek my life, to take it away.

I know during my hardships, this is all I wanted to do. I wanted to go away somewhere and sleep. I felt alone and asked *"Where are your people Lord? Look at what they are doing!"*

It was then that God responded to me like He did with Elijah in the next few verses.

1 Kings 19:18
Yet I have left me seven thousand in Israel, all the knees which have not bowed unto Baal, and every mouth which hath not kissed him.

Seven thousand did not bow! Even when Elijah felt all alone, the Lord had His people in position.

This is a word for us today! The Lord has His people in position. Praise God, we must be encouraged that we are not alone. God's people are here. We must be confident that wherever we are now in our walk, He is continuing to prepare and shape us for His purpose. Just continue to do what you have been called to do!

Matthew 10:28
"And fear not them which kill the body, but are not able to kill the soul: but rather fear him which is able to destroy both soul and body in hell."

"Lord, I will take this stand and trust you all the way. I will do what you call me to do. I love you and know that you are working out good things for me and my family"

Friday, April 13, 2006

My divorce papers arrived in the mail. I was now a divorcee.

It wasn't how I thought things would end, but I had to give it to the Lord. I thank the Lord for giving me the grace to come through this. I know everything will turn for the glory of God. Through this, however, I have matured and have grown more in the things of the Lord. I have had my eyes opened – although this whole ordeal was painful, it was not in vain. The things I have learned couldn't have been taught to me in any Bible college or by anyone else. I believe what I know now has saved my life and will save many more. I know that, one at a time, my family and many others will be saved.

Romans 5:19
"For as by one man's disobedience many were made sinners, so by the obedience of one shall many be made righteous."

Christ's only desire is to have you and to give life to you more abundantly.

No matter who you are, or what you have done, the Lord desires to have you. All he is looking for is someone who is willing, who loves Him, who will give Him their all, who is hungry, and someone who will not compromise. That someone is you!

No matter where you are, no matter how difficult the situation, the Lord is able to take you out and take you through. If you know the Lord, and you live for Him, and you find yourself in a troublesome situation, trust the Lord. He is about to show you some powerful things.

If you don't know God and desire to know Him, He will come wherever you are and guide you out from where you are. All you need to do is call on His name. Sometimes our circumstances will place us up against a wall and at the end of ourselves before we call unto Him. No matter what we may feel and see, the Lord has something planned for us. It is not the crowd we need to please and follow. It doesn't matter what the people around us will say. Sometimes we become so consumed by and concerned with what others may think toward us. But the only thing that matters is what God thinks of us.

All the good things He has done in my life, He can and will do for you. He has brought healing and great joy in my heart. I used to wonder how men and women could just go and give everything up to become missionaries. Well, now I know. The world is all about self, but the Lord is always about others. Giving it all up for Him is worth it and more. How great He is and wonderful; I love Him with all my heart. He desires to be a part of your life too. I think about the life of a man of God in the Bible, David. He knew many heartaches and disappointments. He experienced the loss of a child, a son turned on him, and his own king tried to kill him. And through it all he wrote the following:

Psalm 150:6
Let every thing that hath breath praise the LORD. Praise ye the LORD.

David loved the Lord and no matter what happened, the Lord sustained him.

My Prayer to the Lord

I come to you with thanksgiving. I sit here before you in awe of your goodness. I love you Lord with all my heart. Let the contrite heart be restored and may you hear every cry. Create in me a clean heart and renew a right spirit within me, I sing to you a new song. My heart flows with fresh words and songs only for you.

Lord, you've healed and touched my broken heart and loved me when I wasn't much to love. May my words and my heart be always acceptable in your sight. You're my Friend, my Healer, and my Everything. May the hearers hear what the Spirit of the Lord is saying and draw near. This place is not our home, we are only passing through. The Lord will hold us in His hands and never forsake us. Though darkness may increase, You will continue to sustain us. I love you Lord.

When you don't know how to pray, just open your heart and talk with Him. He already knows what's there, but it's faith that pleases Him. All He waits for from you is your invitation. He sees your pain. He sees the things you have hidden away. He is patient, kind, and merciful. He sends His love and power and, in time, He will change you. He wants to come and live within your heart. His Word is a lamp unto our feet. Humility and submission will usher us to places we never thought we would reach.

He shields and protects us as He watches us grow. Every breath we take is from Him and He loves us more than we could ever know. He is the knight in shining armour I dreamt about. One day soon, He will return.

The wrath of satan is being poured out. Many more people will succumb to suicide. Many more will be murdered. And many more will endure terrible suffering. But it is the hand of the Lord that stretches forth and reaches out to the lost, the suffering, and the dying. There is not one person that He does not see. There is not one person that He is not moved with compassion for.

When there comes a stirring in your heart, a yearning to know Him, know that this is from the Lord. He desires to come into your life. It is by no coincidence you are reading this testimony of what God can do in someone else's life. He desires to walk with you all the days of your life. We can not make this life journey on our own. Sin, especially in our life, brings disease to everything it touches.

Satan is not omniscient. He does not know the specific plans Christ has for you. But he does know that Christ loves you and, if you accept Jesus Christ into your heart, has a planned end in heaven for you. Satan will do everything in his power to make you believe his lies to keep you from God's plan for your life. The biggest lie he uses is that there is no God. If he can get you to believe this lie, then you are missing the most incredible amazing thing you can ever experience. *Ever wonder why it is such a battle for you to believe in Christ?*

If we give our adversary, the devil, a foothold in our lives he will come and destroy every good thing in our lives given to us by God. We must take a stand! We must learn the Word of the Lord and be aware of all His promises and benefits. We must stand in the gap for our family, our marriages, our businesses, and our relationships. Our enemy hates unity and he will divide a house if given the opportunity to do so. He will spare no mercy! We need to be equipped to fight him. We must put on the full armour of the Lord. I encourage you to read and study the entire sixth chapter of Ephesians.

All that we endure for the Lord is to mature us so that our faith becomes unshakeable. The Lord is always building; we are His Body and Christ is building His Church. He is returning for a bride without spot or wrinkle!

He hears the hearts of the single parents. He hears the battle and loves you right where you are.

I praise Him daily for hearing me. I praise Him for saving my children. This is how I know that He hears the hearts of the single parents. He desires to come and lead the broken family and He is the only one able to come and heal and give direction. He feels and grieves for the lost. His heart's only desire is for you to call on His name.

I knew that without God, life would be empty. I knew that my life, and my children's lives, would be empty without Christ. *I didn't want this for me or for my children. I didn't want this emptiness anymore. I had had enough! I despised who I had become.*

I know the fear of being alone. I was afraid of raising my children without their dad; afraid of going through the court system and fighting for custody. I know the fear of losing your child, and the fear of something tragic happening.

Maybe you're a single father and your heart burns because the mother has up and left. Maybe the woman you thought you knew became someone else. Maybe the person you thought you married deceived you and now you are watching someone horrific emerge.

Being a single parent is not easy. It comes with a lot of fears and a lot of heartbreak. One of the hardest things we will do in life is to bring up our children. But we are not alone, unless we refuse Christ. By accepting Christ I know my children can now have a key to eternal life in Jesus Christ. Since I have accepted the Lord and Saviour Jesus Christ into my life, He has walked with me all the way.

I encourage you, seek the Lord while He may be found. Jesus cares for every part of your life, and He will come and show you the way. It was on my knees in prayer that the Lord would strengthen me and give me wisdom. Where I was angry or short with my children, Christ would come in and fill me with love!

It is a comfort to know that Christ loves our children more than we do. He created our children and He desires for all of them to come to Him. They belong to Him and we have been given blessings to train them up in His ways. We will be held accountable by Him if we do not. Single parents, when the kids get sick or afraid, you are not alone. Jesus Christ will be there for you. He is our Protector, our Provider, our Comforter and He is always faithful.

The Lord shows His love in so many ways. We just need to wait on Him and obey Him. Although my children do not have a natural father figure in the home, they have the Heavenly Father. I know the Lord has already prepared a way for them. Our Heavenly Father is all that we need; He leads and provides all the time. Single families, the Lord has made a way for you and your children. Do not be under condemnation for anything. I believe the Lord is raising up single moms and dads for a testimony. When someone we love fails us – and they will fail you – the Lord will come alongside you and lead you and give you great victories. In Him, you, and your children, shall do many great things.

Christ is looking for a people who will love and honour Him. He is building a Church. He will lay a solid foundation for those who will hearken to His voice. He is the Rock upon which the Church is built.

The storms of life are becoming worse each day. They will continue to intensify, but those who build their house on the Word will not be shaken – no matter what we go through! Jesus is always faithful and He will come in to your life and guide you through every storm. He will direct you and lead you. That does not mean that everything will be smooth sailing – it will not! You will endure hardships and you will go through storms, but the Lord will lift you above them. In the midst of the storm you will have unspeakable peace in your heart. When others come at you, He will fill your heart with an amazing love. The Lord does not give as the world gives. His gifts are precious and everlasting. You can trust Him. With Him, you will never be left alone.

There is life after death; our spirit and the choice we make will determine where we will go. I know that in obedience I will preach the gospel in truth. I do this because I love Him, I love you, and I do not want any blood on my hands. The Lord loves all. He does not esteem anyone over another. Don't believe the lie that you are no one or that you cannot do anything. The Lord is just waiting for you to say 'Yes' to Him. Once you do, He will lead you forth to bring you out as a living testimony.

I have a prayer here for those who want to receive Christ into their lives. When you pray, speak from your heart. Remember, the Lord is faithful, He will hear you.

Heavenly Father, I desire to know you. I'm sorry for the things I've done and the things I've said. Forgive me Lord for all of my sins. Wash me and cleanse me from every filthy stain of sin. I believe You died on the cross and that You were raised from the dead. I believe that You are alive forever more. I ask You to come into my life and into my heart. I believe now in the name of Jesus with all my heart. I believe that I have been forgiven and set free. I believe that I am saved.

In the Name of Jesus, Amen.

All of heaven rejoices over one sinner that repents of sin and comes to the Lord Jesus Christ!

CPSIA information can be obtained
at www.ICGtesting.com
Printed in the USA
BVHW080900160721
611883BV00001B/1